CU00871916

The Young Gardener

The Young Gardener

Gardener

The Complete Guide to Gardening for Children

CLARE BRADLEY

Illustrated by Lucy Su

metro

Thanks to all the young gardeners I've met, whose energy
and enthusiasm is inspiring.

And thanks to Henry, Zenna and Akyni
for proving to me that you're never too young
or too old to catch the gardening bug!

First published in Great Britain in 1999
by Metro Books (an imprint of Metro Publishing Limited),
19 Gerrard Street, London W1V 7LA

Editorial and design by Brown Packaging Books Limited,
Bradley's Close, 74-77 White Lion Street, London N1 9PF

British Library Cataloguing in Publication Data.
A CIP record of this book is available on request
from the British Library.

ISBN 1 900512 11 4

10 9 8 7 6 5 4 3 2 1

Project Editor: Nina Hathway
Design: Robert Mathias, Publishing Workshop
Back cover photograph: Amanda Searle/Channel 5

Printed in Italy

Contents

Introduction

A word from Clare

The thrill of seeing tiny seedlings emerge or a little green shoot develop fat, healthy roots is one of the greatest pleasures for me.

If you have never grown anything before, you are in for a real treat, and lucky to start young. I didn't start gardening until I was in my early twenties, how I wish it had been when I was much younger because there is so much to discover. The world of plants is huge and varied and so incredible that it will keep you fascinated for a lifetime.

Never be afraid to experiment and grow plants in your own way, there are no set rules in gardening. You will find that some of the most unlikely schemes will work out brilliantly and those you thought would be perfect may fail. The only thing guaranteed is that you will never stop learning and being amazed at the natural world around you. So don't waste any more time, sow some seeds today that will grow into plants to make your corner of the world a greener, happier and healthier place.

Clare Bradley

x

The best hobby in the world

Nothing compares with the thrill of growing things, and you are helping the Earth by making your patch green and beautiful.

Planting seeds and watching them grow, flower and fruit is the most exciting thing in the world.

Gardening is a challenge, so don't be downhearted if you have failures – we all do – but the pleasure of seeing just one seedling shooting up is worth all the effort.

▷ Hippeastrum grow from bulbs and have big, bright flowers on top of a single, thick stem.

▷ Pretty night-scented stocks send out wafts of perfume in the dark.

▷ Sunflowers can grow to over 4m (13ft) tall.

Plants are always full of surprises. Flowers might be bigger or brighter than you ever thought possible. Some flowers may do something special, like only make perfume at night, or they may grow much taller or fatter than you expected.

If you haven't grown anything before, don't worry, just have a go. You might like to grow a plant from a cutting ...

... or you could even try planting a tree.

Or you could care for a cactus. There are thousands of plants waiting for the chance of a life with you.

Even with just one plant you can do interesting things like watching a fruit develop from a flower. Gardening can open up a whole new world of possibilities.

You could begin with just a single geranium in a pretty pot, keeping it outside in summer ...

... and on a windowsill indoors in winter.

Why gardening is the best hobby in the world

You won't be short of gifts for friends, you can grow your own.
You can be a gardener anywhere, even without a garden.
You can really impress your friends and family.
The more you grow, the better it gets.
You can grow delicious things to eat.
It doesn't have to cost much money.
You can do it alone or with friends.
It is good for the environment.
You can start at any age.
It lasts a lifetime.

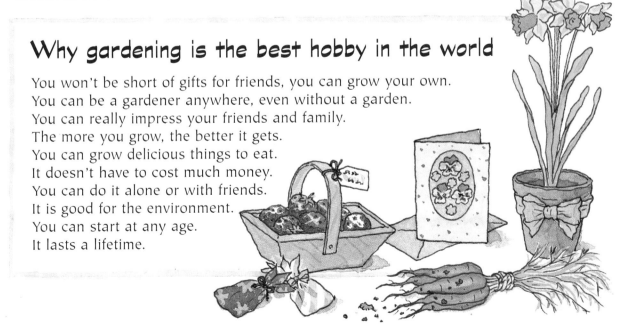

Natural cycle

All nature - from animals and insects to plants and the soil - works together to create a natural cycle of events and a healthy environment. Here's how that cycle works.

Living layers

All life that lives on land depends on soil, which is just a thin layer on the outside of the Earth. Soil is made of extremely small pieces of ground-up rock mixed with dead plants and animals.

Roots push through the soil searching for food and water. They create air spaces that allow small, air-breathing animals, such as insects and bacteria, to live there, too. You cannot see bacteria, but they are very important to the soil. Bacteria decay dead plants and animals. There are millions of bacteria in just one teaspoon of soil.

▽ Animal droppings and the remains of dead plants and animals, are taken into the soil by insects and worms.

Plants feed animals

Animals manure the land

▽ The top-soil is the first layer. It is dark in colour, healthy and full of life.

Roots

Soil feeds plants

Manure feeds the soil

▷ The sub-soil is the second layer which is usually lighter in colour. Sub-soil contains less animal life and plant foods, so it is less fertile than topsoil and not suitable for the roots of plants.

▷ The third layer is rock, the original material that was used to make the soil, thousands of years ago.

How do plants grow?

Animals need to eat food, but green plants can make their own.

Sun

Leaves are green because they contain a chemical called chlorophyll.

Oxygen

Carbon dioxide

Oxygen

As they make food plants give out oxygen.

Carbon dioxide

Leaves absorb carbon dioxide from the air.

Animals breathe out carbon dioxide which plants use to make food.

In sunshine, chlorophyll turns water from the roots and carbon dioxide from the air into energy that helps the plant to grow.

Water

▷ Roots take up water and minerals from the soil.

Trees are so large, they release a lot of oxygen, and that is why forests are often described as the lungs of the earth.

▷ Trees are habitats, which means they are homes for other plants and animals. An oak tree may have 400 species living on it.

What plants need to grow

To make sure plants grow well in your garden, remember how nature does it and try to copy the ideas on a smaller scale.

Some plants are happy in shade, but most like plenty of light. Since some plants need warmth more than others, be sure to read about each one and plant it at the right time of year, when there is enough sun.

Keep indoor plants on a sunny windowsill, but don't let them get too dry.

△ Livingstone daisies love the sun. They open their petals wide when the sun shines, but close up if the sun goes away.

Outside, plant in the sun if you can. If your garden is shady, buy shade-loving plants.

△ Lilies of the valley like to be cool, damp and shady.

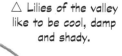

▽ When you water, give plants a good soaking.

Water

Seeds need water to germinate (start growing) and plants need water to keep growing. In nature, rainfall can be a hit and miss affair, but in the garden you can give plants a drink in dry weather.

Take special care of plants growing in pots. Check them every day, as they dry out very quickly in hot or windy weather.

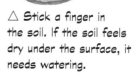

△ Stick a finger in the soil. If the soil feels dry under the surface, it needs watering.

Food

Plant foods are called nutrients. There are already lots of them in your garden soil. You can provide more by adding fertilizer or compost (See pages 22 and 25.)

Air

Plants need air just like you do, but they breathe through their leaves and roots. Leaves can always get enough air, but roots need to grow in crumbly, loose soil with air pockets around the soil particles. Don't trample the soil around plants too much, as it squeezes out the air.

Clare's tip

Never work on the garden if the soil sticks to your boots. When the soil is very wet, your weight can squash the soil so tight that there is no air left for the plants.

How plants drink water

Cut flowers and other plants can survive in water for a few days. Try this experiment to see how a plant sucks up water from its roots.

◁ ▷ The red petals and leaves show that the dyed water has been sucked up through the roots and spread all around the plants.

▷ A white carnation is a good flower to use.

Put a few drops of red food dye into a jug of water.

Put a white flower and a celery stick into the jug.

▽ The white flower will have red-tinged petals.

Leave them for a few hours then look again.

▽ A red spot in the stem shows where it has sucked the water up.

Slice across the celery stem. What do you see?

Useful tools

These are some of the tools you will find useful in the garden. You don't need to buy them all at once. Wait until you need them, or borrow them from someone. Always make sure that a tool is not too big or heavy for you before you buy it.

A spade is for digging over the soil and making holes to plant trees and shrubs. A standard spade is too big for small people, so use a border spade instead.

A hand trowel and fork are like mini spades and forks. They are the most useful tools of all.

A hoe is for speedy weeding. It slices under roots so weeds shrivel and die.

Use a fork to loosen soil and add compost or manure. A border fork is small and easy to use.

A rake breaks up soil and levels the surface.

▷ Garden twine is soft so it doesn't cut into stems.

◁ Gloves protect your hands from sharp things and keep them clean.

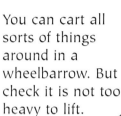

Secateurs are gardeners' scissors. Use them to cut stems or branches.

A seed tray is for sowing seeds and rooting cuttings.

Carry soil in a bucket.

You use potting compost for plants in pots. It is better than normal soil.

You can cart all sorts of things around in a wheelbarrow. But check it is not too heavy to lift.

Be tidy and sweep up after yourself with a broom.

Watering is very important. Choose a watering can with a rose (sprinkler) on the spout to create a gentle shower.

Other useful things are gloves, penknife, twine, scissors and bamboo canes.

Garden plot

Your garden doesn't have to be big, so don't try to make it in the overgrown, shady patch at the bottom of the garden that nobody has been able to grow anything in. If that's the only place you can use, it might be better to start a collection of plants in containers. (Read more about this on page 18.)

Preparing your plot

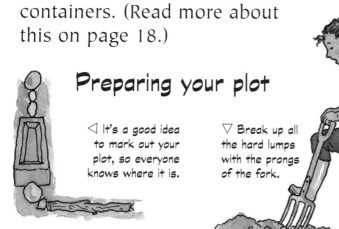

◁ It's a good idea to mark out your plot, so everyone knows where it is.

▽ Break up all the hard lumps with the prongs of the fork.

Work backwards away from the patch you've dug so you don't tread on the freshly-dug part.

Mark out your plot using anything suitable, such as large stones, logs or bricks.

Starting at the back and working roughly in rows, fork over the soil, pulling out the weeds as you go.

Carefully fork over the soil again. Make sure you turn the soil to a depth of about 30cm (1ft).

▽ You can get compost from garden centres.

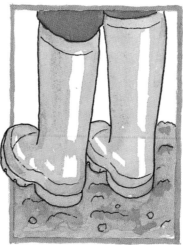

◁ Walk with your weight on your heels.

Spread about 5cm (2in) of compost or manure (see page 22) onto the soil, then mix it in with a fork.

Walk over the plot up and down just once, starting at the back. This gets rid of any bumps and hollows.

Use a rake slowly and carefully to create a level surface. Then your garden is ready for planting.

Making a path

To avoid walking over your beautifully prepared soil, make a path around it.

▽ You can buy bark in large bags from garden centres.

▽ 0.5m (1ft 8in) is usually wide enough.

Decide how wide you want your path to be, then mark it out clearly using small sticks as pegs.

Firm the path by pressing it down with your heels. Walk all over it as many times as you like.

The path now needs a covering; chopped bark looks great. Other ideas are sawdust or gravel.

THE IDEAL SPOT

The ideal spot gets plenty of sun.

It has nice crumbly soil.

It is close to a water tap.

It is at least 1 metre square (1 sq yd).

It is not near large trees or shrubs.

A picket fence

If you're ambitious, and have the space to make a garden that is between 3 and 5 sq m (3.5 and 6 sq yd), the most fabulous boundary of all is a small picket fence. You could ask for one as a birthday present!

▽ Picket fences can be painted white or any other colour.

Container gardening

I f you don't have a garden, the good news is that you can still garden by growing plants in containers. Almost anything that is able to hold potting compost and has holes in the bottom will do nicely.

◁ A great first-time garden is a wooden half-barrel. It's the right size and shape, and big enough for a good display of different plants.

◁ A chimney pot looks interesting. To avoid having to fill the whole pot with potting compost, find a small pot that sits comfortably on top and put your plants in that instead.

△ Old tyres make brilliant containers and you can get them free from most garages. A stack of two or three tyres is a good depth. Stuff the insides of the tyres with straw so it takes less compost to fill the stack. Make the tyres stand out by painting them with bright emulsion paint.

▷ Use an unusual container, such as an old kettle, as a holder. Put in a single plant, such as a fern or trailing geranium.

△ A windowbox makes excellent use of a windowsill or indoor spot. It is either made of clay or plastic. For outside windowsills, clay is better because it's heavier and less likely to blow off.

▽ Flower pots are either clay or plastic, too. Clay pots are more expensive. Plants growing in them need more watering since water evaporates through the clay.

◁ Plastic pots need less watering and are cheaper. They are also lighter so they are easier to carry around. They can look great painted a bright colour, or with trailing plants tumbling over the sides.

Clare's tip

Many composts are still made of peat, which comes from peat bogs. Peat bogs are special places, where rare and wonderful plants grow. The bogs are getting smaller as peat is dug out of them to sell to gardeners. To help preserve peat bogs, look out for peat-free composts, or for those made from coconut fibre, or coir.

Planting containers

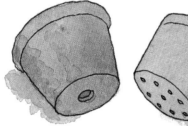

All containers must have drainage holes. Most will have holes already, but if you use a holder that doesn't, you'll need to make some. If it's too hard to do yourself, ask an adult to help you.

Containers need something in the bottom to stop the drainage holes getting blocked with soil. Use broken bits of clay pots or flat stones. For large pots, broken pieces of polystyrene are an ideal material.

Because plants growing in pots are in a restricted place, it is important that they have something top-class to put their roots in. Garden soil is hardly ever good enough. Instead, buy a bag of potting compost from a garden centre.

Weeding

Weeds are any plants growing where you don't want them. When they grow in a hedgerow or roadside verge people call them wildflowers, but in the garden they are bullies that crowd plants and steal their light and water. Weeds are very strong and that is why they are so successful.

Weeding rules

Make it a habit to weed your garden often, pulling weeds out when they are still very young, before they flower. Use a bucket or container to collect up weeds. Knock as much soil off them as you can. Then you can either throw the weeds away or pile them out of sight, sheltered from rain, while you persuade your parents to have a bonfire. Don't add weeds to the compost bin as they will grow and flourish there.

Clare's tip

Did you know that weeds can live for years in the soil? There's a saying that goes, 'one year's seeding, seven years' weeding' – and it's true. Remind yourself of this when you don't feel like weeding. When you plant seeds in the garden, sow them in straight lines and use labels to mark the rows. This makes it easier to see which plants to keep and which to pull out.

◁ If it's outside a row, it's probably a weed.

Some common weeds

△ Bindweed (*Convolvulus arvensis*)

▷ Couch grass (*Agropyron repens*)

Couch grass, bindweed and ground elder are hard to get rid of. They have long roots and can grow again from a piece left in the ground, so dig every bit out.

▷ Ground elder (*Aegopodium podagraria*)

◁ Spear thistle (*Cirsium vulgare*)

Ouch! the leaves of this weed are sharply pointed and have spines, too. The flowers produce hundreds of seeds.

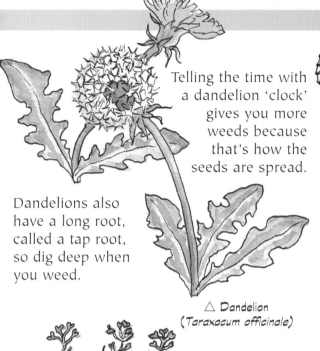

Telling the time with a dandelion 'clock' gives you more weeds because that's how the seeds are spread.

Dandelions also have a long root, called a tap root, so dig deep when you weed.

△ Dandelion
(*Taraxacum officinale*)

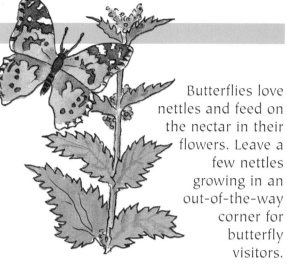

Butterflies love nettles and feed on the nectar in their flowers. Leave a few nettles growing in an out-of-the-way corner for butterfly visitors.

△ **Nettle (*Urtica dioica*)**

You've all felt the stinging hairs of this weed, so wear gloves when you handle it. At least nettles are quite easy to pull up.

This is very fast growing. Each plant can produce up to 4,000 seeds a year and each seed can survive in the soil for up to 30 years!

◁ Shepherd's purse
(*Capsella bursa-pastoris*)

Mulching

A mulch is like a blanket you put on to cover the soil around plants. It helps to stop weeds growing and keeps the soil moist and soft under-neath. To work really well the mulch should be at least 5cm (2in) thick - and the thicker the better.

△ Bark: Chopped bark can be bought in large bags at garden centres. The rougher the cut, the longer it will last.

▷ Groundsel
(*Senecio vulgaris*)

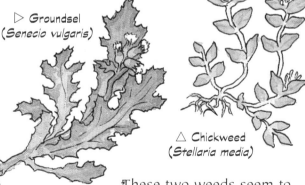

△ Chickweed
(*Stellaria media*)

These two weeds seem to pop up all over the place and they grow quickly, but they are quite easy to pull up.

△ Woodchips: Made from chipped and shredded tree branches. You might get some cheap, or even free, if you contact your local tree surgeon.

△ Straw: Good for large plants such as marrows and pumpkins, and for strawberry plants. To stop straw blowing all over the place, water well after you have laid it.

Making good soil

The basis of good gardening is to create healthy, rich soil. In nature, dead and rotting plants and animal manure feed the soil. In a garden, you often take dead plants away so you have to put something back into the soil yourself. The stuff you need for this job is garden compost, leaf-mould or manure. You will find out about each of these here.

Compost

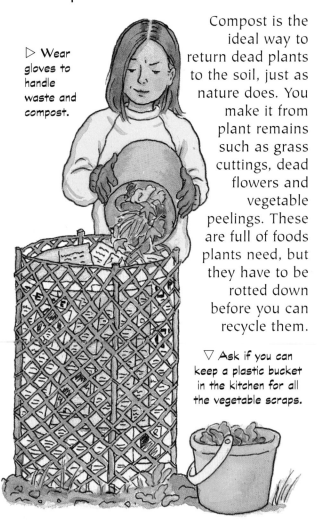

▷ Wear gloves to handle waste and compost.

Compost is the ideal way to return dead plants to the soil, just as nature does. You make it from plant remains such as grass cuttings, dead flowers and vegetable peelings. These are full of foods plants need, but they have to be rotted down before you can recycle them.

▽ Ask if you can keep a plastic bucket in the kitchen for all the vegetable scraps.

△ Plant remains rot faster if you fill the bin in one go. Mix the remains before you squash them down.

Making a compost bin

Take a piece of wire or plastic netting and tie it together with string to make a cylinder.

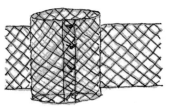

Thread at least four bamboo canes through the netting. Space them evenly around the cylinder.

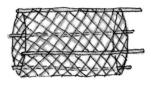

Stick the canes into the ground so they hold the netting upright and anchor it securely.

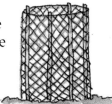

Line the bin all the way up the sides with plenty of sheets of old newspaper.

Draw and cut out a circle for a lid from a piece of cardboard. Put it into a plastic bag to keep out the rain.

About your bin

WHAT TO PUT IN
Old flowers, soft plant stems, straw, vegetable peelings, fruit skins, crushed egg shells, tea bags, lawn mowings (never make a thick layer of these, mix them in with other things).

LEAVE OUT
Cooked food, weeds, tough stems or sticks, leaves (use fallen leaves separately to make leaf-mould – see right).

HOW LONG DOES IT TAKE?
Compost is made faster in warm weather when it is ready to use in about 12 weeks. In colder weather it takes longer.

SHRINKING COMPOST
After a few weeks you will be surprised to find the compost has shrunk. Don't worry – the bacteria that rot the plant remains have been working hard. Then you can add some more garden waste.

Leaf-mould

Leaves take longer to rot down than garden compost because of their tough skeletons. Be prepared to wait at least a year, possibly even two. But the wonderful, crumbly compost is worth waiting for. In fact, leaf-mould is so good that you can use it as compost for potting or sowing seeds.

Manure

Animal manure is the best stuff you could wish for on your soil, so it is worth making a trip to your local riding stables. However, it should not be

used straight away, but stored for about eight weeks, either in plastic bags with air-holes, or as a pile in the corner of the garden. You can also buy bags of very rich, concentrated manure from garden centres – this is powerful stuff so use carefully.

Making a wormery

Earthworms in garden soil recycle dead plants, leaves and animals (see page 10). There is another type of worm, called the Brandling or Tiger, which you can keep in your garden in a wormery to make compost. Here's how to make a wormery.

First you need to get hold of a small plastic dustbin. Ask an adult to help you drill two rows of drainage holes 2.5cm (1in) from the bottom.

Next drill another row of air holes around near the top edge. Put in a layer of gravel. Cut a circle of plastic (from a black bin liner, for example). Punch holes in the plastic and place it on the gravel. Then add a 10cm (4in) layer of potting compost. Now you can introduce the worms to their new home. Let them settle for a day or two, then put in a thin layer of vegetable waste.

Worms love:	Worms hate:
TEA-BAGS	ORANGE AND LEMON PEEL
BANANAS	
POTATO PEEL	ONION SKINS
CARROT SKIN	
BRUSSEL SPROUTS	TOUGH STALKS

▽ The worms will eat their way to the top of the pile, turning your rubbish into wonderful compost on the way.

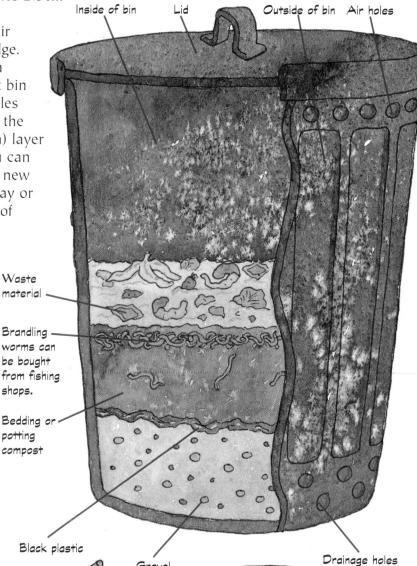

Inside of bin   Lid   Outside of bin   Air holes

Waste material

Brandling worms can be bought from fishing shops.

Bedding or potting compost

Black plastic

Gravel

Drainage holes

Feeding plants

As well as air and water, plants also need minerals from the soil. Plants in soil outdoors have enough to eat if you have added compost or manure, but extra food given as a fertilizer can give plants a boost. Plants in pots always need feeding because they grow in a small space. Potting compost contains food at first, but plants use it up and need fertilizer.

Clare's tip

There are many types of fertilizers. The label will say which type of plant a fertilizer is best for. Choose one for leaves or flowers, or a good all-round one that has everything.

Fertilizer fact file

What do plants need?

Plants use many different minerals in tiny amounts, but they need large helpings of three main ones – nitrogen, phosphorus and potassium.

◁ Potassium (K) to help produce flowers and fruit.

◁ Nitrogen (N) to help leaves grow.

◁ Phosphorus (P) for healthy roots.

How often?

As a general rule, most plants need feeding about every three weeks during the growing season. Hungry plants or pots crowded with flowers need feeding as often as once a week.

▷ Tomato plants growing in pots need feeding every week.

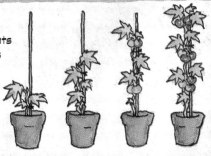

How do you use them?

Dilute liquid fertilizers by adding one glug to a full watering can.

◁ Sprinkle fertilizer granules around a plant, then gently fork them into the soil.

All about seeds

Many flowering plants make seeds which, if they are lucky, will grow into new plants. Growing plants from seeds is one of the most exciting parts of gardening. You can save money, too, if you collect your own seeds every season.

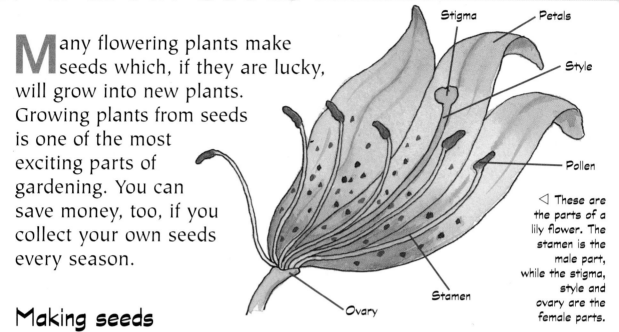

Stigma — Petals

Style

Pollen

◁ These are the parts of a lily flower. The stamen is the male part, while the stigma, style and ovary are the female parts.

Stamen

Ovary

Making seeds

Each flower's male and female parts are protected by petals. For a plant to make seeds, the pollen from the male part has to reach the ovary of the female part. This process is called pollination. See how it happens below.

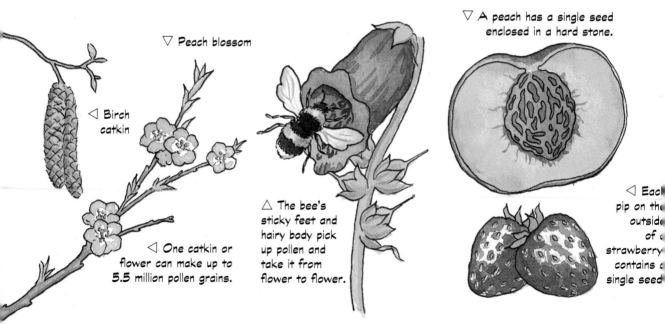

▽ Peach blossom

◁ Birch catkin

◁ One catkin or flower can make up to 5.5 million pollen grains.

△ The bee's sticky feet and hairy body pick up pollen and take it from flower to flower.

▽ A peach has a single seed enclosed in a hard stone.

◁ Each pip on the outside of a strawberry contains a single seed

Some plants produce masses of pollen. It is so light that it is blown from flower to flower.

Usually insects move pollen around from plant to plant – bees and butterflies, for example.

After pollination, a fruit develops around the seeds to protect them and keep them safe as they grow.

Seed collecting

Let seeds ripen on the plant until the pod is brown and dry. Collect them in a paper bag.

If the pods are damp, lay them in a warm room until dry.

Twist the seeds from the pods, put them in envelopes and write the name and date on each.

△ Seeds are usually dark brown or black.

Lay pods on a tray.

Seed sowing

When seeds are buried in soil and watered they begin to swell. A baby plant bursts out of each one and this is called germination.

▽ A small root appears first and grows downwards.

▷ Then a leafy shoot pushes up into the light.

Sowing indoors

Many garden flowers come from places where it is warm all year. In colder climates these must be started off indoors and only planted outside when there is no danger of frosts. You can use any container as long as it holds potting compost and you can make holes in the bottom for drainage.

▽ Use a flat hand, like this.

Fill a small pot with seed or potting compost. Overfill it, then wipe off the extra.

With a small, flat-bottomed pot, press the surface down a little to make it level.

▷ Cover so that you just cannot see the seeds any more.

Sow the seeds about 1cm (½in) apart. Cover with a little compost.

Stand the pot in a bowl of water for about 15 minutes to soak water up into it.

◁ Pull out weaker plants. Less than 2.5cm (1in) apart is too close.

When the seeds sprout, put them in a sunny spot. If too many grow, pull some out.

Moving seedlings

◁ A dibber is a tool for making holes. You can use a twig or ice cream stick instead.

Instead of thinning (see page 27), you can move the seedlings into a bigger pot while they are still small, as shown below. Prepare a container as for sowing seeds (see page 27). Use a dibber to make holes in the compost about 5cm (2in) apart.

Use the dibber to lever out a few seedlings. Hold the seedling by the round seed-leaf, not the stem.

▷ This makes them grow bushy.

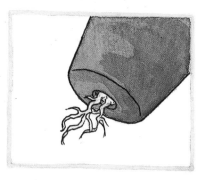

Place each seedling in a hole and, with the dibber, lightly press a little compost against the roots. Water and put in a light place.

When the seedlings are a few centimetres tall, pinch out the top pair of leaves. Pinch the stem just where the leaves join.

When small white roots grow right through the holes in the pot, the young plants are ready to be taken outside.

▷ While you wait, decide where to put your plants and prepare the soil (page 22).

Leave the seedlings in their pots outside for a few days, to get used to the great outdoors.

Clare's tip

If the seedlings grow too tall and thin, they may lack light. Take a piece of cardboard that is taller and wider than the pot and paint one side white. Fold it, then stand behind the pot.

△ The white side facing the seedlings reflects extra light onto the plants.

Planting

Before you plant
seedlings out, make sure
the compost in the
pots is moist. If it
needs watering, do this
at least an hour before so
extra water drains away.

Dig a small hole in
the garden with a
trowel. Spread your
fingers around the
plant, turn the pot
upside down and tap
it gently to get the
seedling and soil out.

Put the roots and lower
stem into the hole.
Cover with soil up to
the lowest leaves.
If your hole isn't
big enough, make
it bigger now,
don't scrunch up
the roots.

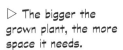
▷ The bigger the
grown plant, the more
space it needs.

Sowing outside

Many seeds can be sown outside, especially
in spring. Check the packet before you plant.

▷ First, fork over
the soil, firm it
and rake it level.
Mark the area
to be sown by
drawing the outline
on the soil with
a stick.

▷ Use the stick
to make seed
drills (grooves in
the soil) about
2cm (¾in) deep.
Make straight
lines about 30cm
(1ft) apart.

▷ Sow the seeds
leaving about 1cm
(½in) between
each. It is better
to sow thinly than
thickly. Cover the
drill with soil and
pat down gently.

▷ The seedlings
will need thinning
out (see page 27)
to leave 10-30cm
(4-12in) between
each one,
depending on the
type of plant.

What are annuals?

Flowers are put into groups according to how they grow, reproduce and die. Many garden flowers are in the group called annuals. These are the quickest to grow because they grow, flower, make seeds and die all in one season.

About annuals

Annuals aim to make as many flowers as they can, in order to attract insects to pollinate them. This means they make lots of seeds to ensure more plants grow. Annuals are cheap to grow as all you need to buy is a packet of seeds, or they are free if you collect the seeds yourself. You can sow them at different times, inside or out, depending on how tough the plant is.

▲ Cosmos
(*Cosmea bipinnatus*)
The Cosmos has fern-like leaves and masses of large, daisy-like flowers in pink, red or white.
How to grow: sow seeds indoors in early spring and put the young plants outside from early summer onwards.
Height: up to 145cm (4ft 10in).
Flowers: in summer.

▶ Sunflower
(*Helianthus annuus*)
These must be top of any list for annuals. The really tall ones are impressive, but smaller ones, or even dwarf ones, may be better in a small garden.
How to grow: in cold regions, sow seeds indoors in spring, one seed per pot. Plant out when about 30cm (1ft) tall. Allow 30cm (1ft) between plants.

▷ If two seedlings germinate, you must move one.

In warmer places, sow seeds outside. Put in a tall, strong stake, then sow two seeds at the bottom.
Height: the tallest reach 3-4m (9-13ft) in just a few months.
Flowers: in summer.

◁ Sweet peas climb on their own, clinging tight with twining tendrils.

▲ Sweet pea
(*Lathyrus odoratus*)
The delicate perfume of the flowers makes this plant a real favourite.
How to grow: soak the seeds overnight before sowing; they have a tough coat and soaking softens it.

◁ Soak the seeds in a jar of water.

Sow in early spring in deep pots, either indoors or outside in a sheltered place. Space plants about 15cm (6in) apart.
Tip: for bushy plants, pinch off the tip of the stem when seedlings are about 10cm (4in) tall.
Height: up to 2.5m (8ft) tall, so they need bamboo canes, netting or trellis to grow up.
Flowers: in summer.

▶ Nasturtium
(*Tropaeolum majus*)
Nasturtiums have squiggly stems and leaves like lily-pads. They have big yellow or orange flowers.

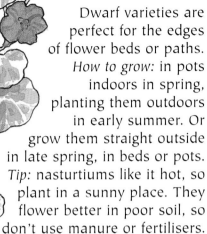

▼ Shirley poppy
(*Papaver rhoeas*)
Comes in shades of pink, white, rose and crimson.
How to grow: plant seeds outside in spring and thin seedlings to 15cm (6in).
Height: up to 60cm (2ft) tall.
Flowers: in summer.

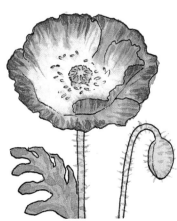

Dwarf varieties are perfect for the edges of flower beds or paths.
How to grow: in pots indoors in spring, planting them outdoors in early summer. Or grow them straight outside in late spring, in beds or pots.
Tip: nasturtiums like it hot, so plant in a sunny place. They flower better in poor soil, so don't use manure or fertilisers.
Height: nasturtiums are naturally trailing plants so they are great for hanging baskets or pots, but they can also climb a wigwam of sticks or a fence, reaching more than 2m (6ft) tall.
Flowers: in summer.

Clare's tip
Gardeners have learned to lengthen the life of annual plants by removing flowers before they make seeds. It's called dead-heading, and, if you do it every few days, plants will go on making flowers for much longer.

▽ Pinch off any dead or dying flowers.

Year after year

Another group of flowers is called perennials. Many garden flowers are in this group. They are called perennials because they grow year after year.

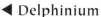
◁ Tie the stems gently to the sticks with garden twine.

◀ **Delphinium**
(*Delphinium elatum*)
These have majestic spires of beautiful flowers. Delphiniums take some trouble to grow well, but are worth it.
How to grow: sow seeds outside in spring or autumn. Or buy plants from garden centres in early summer.

Height: up to 2m (6ft) tall.
Tip: in rain and strong winds the long stems easily fall over so each plant needs staking early in the year. As soon as spring growth starts, use sticks or bamboo canes to support the stems as they grow.
Flowers: in summer.

▼ **Ice plant**
(*Sedum spectabile*)
Ice plants thrive in hot, dry conditions. The flower heads attract butterflies and bees in late summer.
How to grow: The easiest way is to get a bit from a friend who has one.
Height: 30-60cm (1-2ft).
Tip: Even small pieces without roots can grow.
Flowers: in late summer.

▲ **Bleeding heart**
(*Dicentra spectabilis*)
This is one of the first perennials to put its head above ground in spring. Fresh green leaves give way to two-toned flowers shaped like little lockets.
How to grow: they are not easy to grow from seed.

Buy small plants from garden centres in spring.
Tip: they like a slightly shady spot. Make new plants by digging up a large clump and dividing it into smaller plants in autumn or early spring.
Height: about 75cm (2ft 6in).
Flowers: spring and summer.

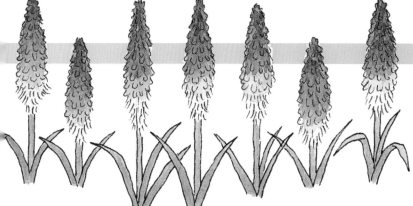

▲ Red hot poker
(*Kniphofia*)

These have grass-like leaves and eye-catching spikes of long, tubular flowers. Choose from bright red, orange or even yellow, but the true colour is red-tipped with a yellow base.

How to grow: they are not easy to grow from seed. Buy small plants in garden centres in early summer.

Tip: very cold winters can damage them. Help to protect the buds by covering with a layer of straw or bracken in late autumn. They like plenty of sunshine and a soil that is not too rich (no need to use fertilizer or manure).

Height: 60cm-1m (2-3ft) tall, but the spikes are sturdy and do not need to be staked.

Flowers: late summer.

▼ Phlox
(*Phlox paniculata*)

This flower is known for its large and impressive flower heads in bright colours.

How to grow: easily grown from seed. Have plants about 45cm (18in) apart.

Tip: Phlox like a moist soil and are best in a sunny or shady spot in the garden.

Height: 60cm-1m (2-3ft).

Flowers: in summer.

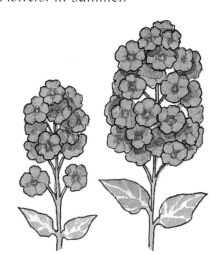

Dividing perennials

Many perennials run out of steam after a few years when the clumps become overcrowded. To give them a new lease of life, lift a whole group of plants with a fork. Divide into pieces – each piece should have three or four shoots and some roots. Throw away any dead bits in the middle. Replant the new plants at least 30cm (12in) apart and water them well.

About perennials

Perennials die down each winter, but spring up again each spring. They start flowering in early summer and carry on until the first frosts of autumn. Perennials are greedy plants that appreciate regular feeding and manuring to keep them healthy and strong.

Taking root

As well as growing from seed, many plants can grow new roots from little bits of themselves, called cuttings. There are three main ways to take cuttings.

Semi-ripe cuttings

Grow new shrubs this way from midsummer to autumn. Look for side shoots up to 15cm (6in) long with no flower buds.

The cutting should be soft and green at the top, but stiffer at the bottom.

Make a straight cut below a leaf joint. Pull the leaves off the bottom half.
Take semi-ripe cuttings from: Butterfly bush (*Buddleia davidii*), cistus, hebe, honeysuckle and weigela.

Softwood cuttings

▽ Side stem

Cut a side stem about 7.5cm (3in) long from fresh, young growth in spring or summer.

◁ Near the leaf joint is where roots are most likely to develop.

Lay the cutting on a flat surface and, with a sharp knife, make a clean cut just below a leaf joint.
Take softwood cuttings from: Pelargonium, fuchsia, campanula, dahlia and chrysanthemum.

Hardwood cuttings

◁ Cut stems that are about 20cm (8in) long and as thick as a pencil.

Cut a woody stem in late autumn. Make a slanting cut just above a bud.

▽ Put the straight end in the soil.

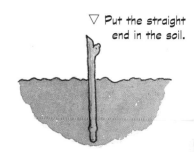

Plant it in a 15cm (6in) hole in the garden, so the top third is above the soil.
Take hardwood cuttings from: Butterfly bush (*Buddleia davidii*), dogwood (*Cornus*), forsythia, mock orange (*Philadelphus*) and flowering currants (*Ribes*).

Planting cuttings

▽ Make holes around the edge of the pot.

Fill a small pot with seed or cuttings compost. Make a hole for each cutting with a pencil.

Cut the leaves off the lower half. Dipping the end into rooting hormone powder can help roots grow.

Put each cutting in a hole, fill the hole with compost and firm it in lightly with the pencil.

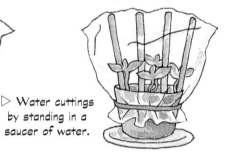

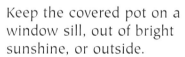

▷ Water cuttings by standing in a saucer of water.

Indoor plants

Here's an easy way to grow cuttings from many indoor plants. Simply pull a healthy leaf off and put the stalk in a jar of water.

Place four canes in the pot cover with a plastic bag. Secure with a rubber band.

Keep the covered pot on a window sill, out of bright sunshine, or outside.

As soon as you see the cuttings start to grow, remove the plastic and put each seedling into its own little pot.

The cutting should develop roots in a couple of weeks. When there are several roots, plant in potting compost.

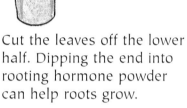

Bulbs

Bulbs are some of the first flowers of the year to appear. They pop up again and again from bulbs hidden underground.

◀ **Daffodils**
(*Narcissus*)
Daffodils are one of the most popular spring bulbs. There are more than 500 types and they are easy to grow.
How to grow: daffodils will grow almost anywhere and should be planted as early as possible in autumn. They can also be grown indoors. Plant in containers, with the bulbs close, but not touching, and the tips just showing above the potting compost. Then treat like hyacinths.
Height: 10cm-60cm (4in-2ft).
Flowers: in mid-spring. The flowers are long lasting.

About bulbs

After flowering the leaves of these plants die down and food is stored in the bulb through the winter. A bulb is really a shoot wrapped up in a thick, white fleshy bulb under the soil. The bulb has a brown, papery tunic and stores enough food to fuel the shoot when it leaps into action in the spring. It is very important to let bulb leaves die down naturally. While they are green they are feeding next year's flower bud inside the bulb.

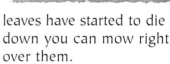

▲ **Crocus**
Most crocuses flower very early in the year, making a splash of colour when little else is out. They are brave little plants that come up year after year.

How to plant: Crocuses look good in containers. Also plant them around perennial plants and shrubs that start growing later in the year, and in grassy areas. Once the

leaves have started to die down you can mow right over them.
Height: about 10cm (4in).
Flowers: in early spring, but crocus flowers don't last long in wind and rain.

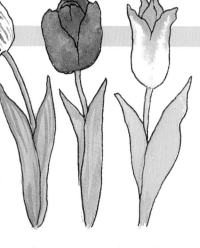

▶ Tulips (*Tulipa*)
Today there are more than 800 different types of tulips to grow.
How to grow: plant in late autumn at least 15cm (6in) deep. Tulips flower best in a sunny spot.
Height: 10cm-1m (4in-3ft).
Tip: always check the height when you buy tulips. Tall ones look silly in a window box and short ones might get lost in the middle of a flower bed.

Flowers: in mid- to late-spring. Colours range from white to almost black, and from softest pink to deep purple. Some have striped, fringed or curled petals.

▷ Don't squeeze the bulb too hard when testing for firmness.

When buying bulbs wear gloves and inspect them carefully. Only choose those bulbs that feel firm, a soft one is likely to be rotten inside.

Each bulb should be planted in a hole that is three times as deep as it is long.

Autumn is the main time for planting bulbs, and most of them grow just as well in pots as in the soil out in the garden.

Use newspaper to keep the hyacinth bulbs dark. Put outside for three or four weeks so roots can grow.

Bring the pot indoors and keep in a light, cool spot until buds grow. Then you can put the pot anywhere.

▲ Hyacinths
Hyacinths can be planted outside to flower in spring, or grown indoors as houseplants.
How to grow: outside, plant bulbs where you want them to grow, in the autumn. Indoors, plant the bulbs in pots in potting compost in late summer or early autumn.

Height: 15-18cm (6-8in).
Flowers: from Christmas onwards. Flowers are long lasting, with a sweet scent.

The pointed end is where the shoot grows from and is called the 'nose' – so plant bulbs nose-up.

Planting shrubs

Shrubs bought in a pot can be planted at almost any time of the year, providing the soil is not frozen, waterlogged or bone dry. Autumn is the best time as plants can settle into their new home over the winter, and shoot up when spring arrives.

Planting step-by-step

Planting shrubs in the spring and summer is fine, as long as you water them well during their first year.

With a spade, dig a hole at least 10cm (4in) bigger than the pot. Loosen the soil at the bottom with a hand fork.

Add a generous helping of compost. Put some in the bottom of the hole and the rest on the soil you have already dug out.

Place the shrub in the hole to check that it is the right size. The top of the pot should be at or just below soil level.

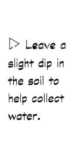

▷ Leave a slight dip in the soil to help collect water.

To ease the plant out, turn it upside down and tap on the pot rim. Don't pull the shrub out by the stem – you might damage it.

Place the shrub in the hole and push the soil back around the roots. Firm the soil down gently as you go. Water well.

Pruning shrubs

Giving plants a good haircut is called pruning. Some shrubs perform better if they are pruned regularly, others don't need pruning at all.

When to prune

The general rule is to prune shrubs after they have flowered. Many types of deciduous shrubs flower best on branches that are at least a year old. If you cut shrubs back straight after flowering, they have a full year to grow and make new flower buds that will bloom next time. This also keeps the bush healthy.

How to prune

Cut back all the shoots that have flowered to a healthy-looking bud. Cut out any thin or spindly shoots right down to ground level.

Cut shoots back to two or three buds from their base. New shoots will then grow and produce flowers. (See exactly how to do it below.)

Which shrubs?

Forsythia
Broom (*Cytisus*)
Kerria
Mock orange (*Philadelphus*)
Bridal wreath (*Spiraea*)
Weigela
Flowering currants (*Ribes*)
Butterfly bush (*Buddleia davidii*)
Fuchsia
Cotton lavender (*Santolina*)

Good pruning

Snip cleanly just above a healthy bud. Don't leave jagged edges or crushed stems. These weaken the plant and let in diseases.

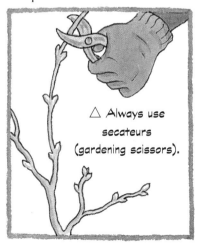

△ Always use secateurs (gardening scissors).

Overgrown shrubs

▽ Cut away the thin tops of branches first.

Pruning a tall, straggly shrub back hard makes the plant look tidier and gives it more energy to flower.

△ With a small pruning saw, or loppers, cut off the branches about 10cm (4in) from the ground.

Beautiful bushes

Gardeners call bushes 'shrubs'. They have a framework of tough, woody stems and live for years. Shrubs often grow large, so read the label carefully.

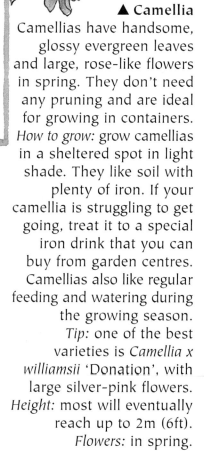

Where to plant shrubs

Shrubs can look interesting all year round with flowers, fruit or autumn colour, or perhaps all three. There are also many that are evergreen and attractive all year round. While shrubs are still small, they look good with bulbs (see page 36), perennials (page 32) or annual flowers (page 30) planted underneath (called underplanting). New shrubs are usually grown from cuttings taken in summer or autumn.

▲ **Camellia**

Camellias have handsome, glossy evergreen leaves and large, rose-like flowers in spring. They don't need any pruning and are ideal for growing in containers.
How to grow: grow camellias in a sheltered spot in light shade. They like soil with plenty of iron. If your camellia is struggling to get going, treat it to a special iron drink that you can buy from garden centres. Camellias also like regular feeding and watering during the growing season.
Tip: one of the best varieties is *Camellia x williamsii* 'Donation', with large silver-pink flowers.
Height: most will eventually reach up to 2m (6ft).
Flowers: in spring.

▲ **Mexican orange blossom**
(*Choisya ternata*)
This is a wonderful plant which grows well in all but the coldest areas. Mexican orange blossom has glossy, evergreen leaves with a spicy scent, but the flowers are its crowning glory. They are purest white and have a sweet fragrance.

How to plant: Mexican orange blossom can be planted in full sun or lightly shaded spots.
Height: up to 2.5m (8ft). If the shrub gets too big, prune the branches after flowering (see page 39).
Flowers: in spring, and again later in mild places.

◁ *Camellia x williamsii 'Donation'*

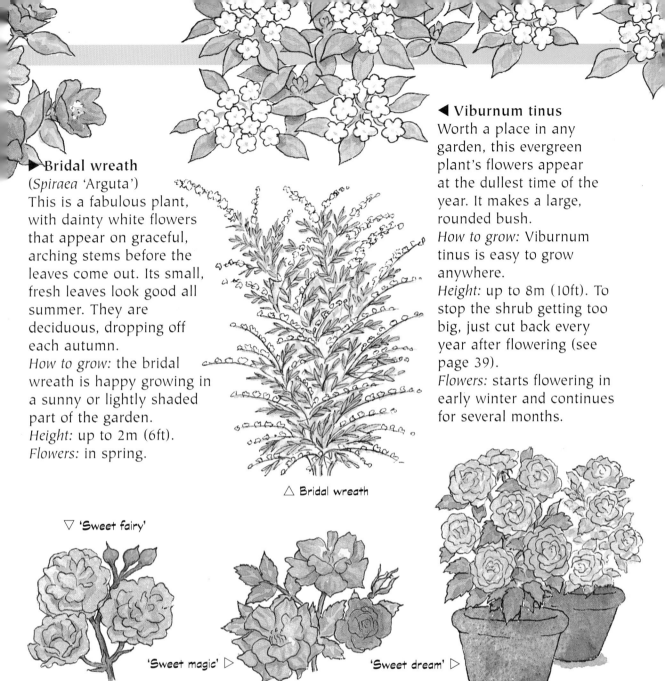

▶ Bridal wreath
(*Spiraea* 'Arguta')
This is a fabulous plant, with dainty white flowers that appear on graceful, arching stems before the leaves come out. Its small, fresh leaves look good all summer. They are deciduous, dropping off each autumn.
How to grow: the bridal wreath is happy growing in a sunny or lightly shaded part of the garden.
Height: up to 2m (6ft).
Flowers: in spring.

△ Bridal wreath

◀ Viburnum tinus
Worth a place in any garden, this evergreen plant's flowers appear at the dullest time of the year. It makes a large, rounded bush.
How to grow: Viburnum tinus is easy to grow anywhere.
Height: up to 8m (10ft). To stop the shrub getting too big, just cut back every year after flowering (see page 39).
Flowers: starts flowering in early winter and continues for several months.

▽ 'Sweet fairy'

'Sweet magic' ▷

'Sweet dream' ▷

▲ Roses (*Rosa*)
There are so many roses to choose from that the choice can be bewildering. Some of the new patio roses are excellent plants – they are small and neat, and flower their hearts out.

How to grow: patio roses are just right for growing in pots, containers or at the front of a flowerbed.
Tips: 'Sweet fairy' is wonderfully scented and bursting with petals. The bright orange petals of

'Sweet magic' fade to a golden yellow colour, and 'Sweet dream' is one of the best patio roses, with clusters of double flowers.
Height: patio roses grow up to 20cm (8in).
Flowers: summer to autumn.

From little acorns

There are thousands of different kinds of trees. Some live for hundreds of years and grow huge, so they are much too big for most gardens. But there are many medium-sized and small trees that are great for normal gardens.

Planting a tree

Sow any seeds you collect from trees outside in small pots of seed compost.

Tie a circle of plastic around the pot. Leave it outside for the winter.

▽ Grow the shoots on for another year before planting in their final position.

Check in spring. When little shoots appear, remove the cover. Keep well watered.

The following autumn, move the seedlings into individual pots.

▲ **Oak** (*Quercus*)
The fruits of the oak are acorns, which are nuts held in a saucerlike cup. Acorns ripen and fall to the ground in autumn after a sharp frost separates each acorn from its cup.

▼ **Pine** (*Pinus*)
Pine tree seeds are in the familiar cones which take two years to ripen. Look for fallen cones that are still closed – the best time is after a windy day. Put them in a box to dry. As they dry they open up and you can get the seeds out.

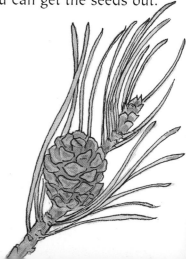

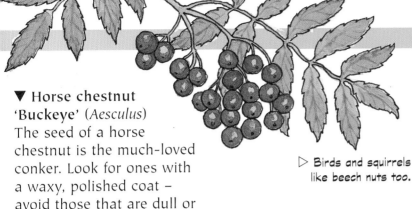

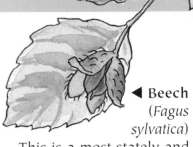

▼ Horse chestnut 'Buckeye' (*Aesculus*)

The seed of a horse chestnut is the much-loved conker. Look for ones with a waxy, polished coat – avoid those that are dull or wrinkled – and sow straight away. Because conkers are such large seeds they need a large pot – an old milk carton with a few drainage holes in the bottom will do.

▷ Birds and squirrels like beech nuts too.

▲ Rowan (*Sorbus*)

The bright-red berries of this tree have seeds inside. Collect them in autumn as soon as they are ripe. Rowan, like many other berries, refuse to germinate until wet weather has softened the seedcoat. To prepare them for winter, squash the berries with something heavy, such as a stone, then mix the crushed berries with a couple of handfuls of sand. Put them in a pot outside. Winter weather will freeze and thaw them. In early spring, tip them out of the pot and sow in pots of compost. You do not have to separate the seed from the sand.

◀ Beech (*Fagus sylvatica*)

This is a most stately and impressive tree. The fruit contains two seeds or 'nuts' which fall to the ground ready to plant. Collect seed from the Copper Beech too. Some seedlings will be green, but one or two may be like their handsome parent.

Did you know?

You can tell the age of an oak tree fairly accurately with the help of a tape measure.

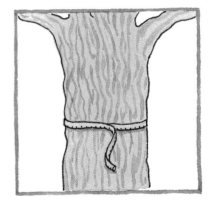

An oak tree gets 2.5cm (1in) fatter every year by adding a new layer of wood under the bark. So if an oak measures 250cm (100in) around the trunk, the tree is 100 years old!

Bark rubbing

The pattern of the bark of a tree is like a fingerprint, each tree has its own pattern. Hold a sheet of thick paper firmly against the trunk and rub over with a thick wax crayon until the bark pattern appears. Try different trees for different designs.

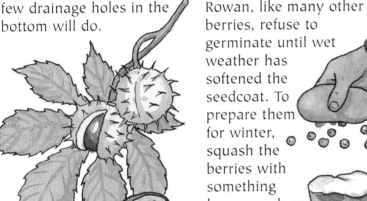

Small trees

Trees are the longest-lived garden plants, so they are something special to grow in your garden. Plant a tree to celebrate a special event, perhaps a birth or an anniversary. Here are some lovely small trees to choose from.

◀ **Kilmarnock willow**
(*Salix caprea 'Pendula'*)
A miniature weeping willow that grows to 1.5-2m (4ft 6in-6ft) tall. It has pussy willow catkins in early spring. The leaves are silky, silver first, turning to silvery green.

◁ Cut off some of the old branches underneath every few years to stop the tree from getting too top heavy.

▶ **Willow-leaved pear**
(*Pyrus salicifolia 'Pendula'*)
This tree has incredible silver leaves which keep their shine all summer long. It also has pure white flowers in spring, which blossom at the same time as the young leaves unfurl. It grows to about 4m (12ft) tall.

▷ Unfortunately, the pears that grow are too hard to eat!

Planting a tree

Dig a hole at least 10cm (4in) deeper than the depth of the tree's pot. Fork over the bottom of the hole, then add manure or compost and fork that in too.

Carefully take the tree out of its pot and position it in the hole checking that the top of the compost is at the same height as the top of the soil.

Put a strong stake (about 1m (3ft) long) into the hole close to the tree's roots and hammer it into place. Leave about 60cm (2ft) above soil level.

Re-fill the hole with the soil that has been dug out, firming gently around the roots. Tie the tree to the stake with part of an old pair of tights.

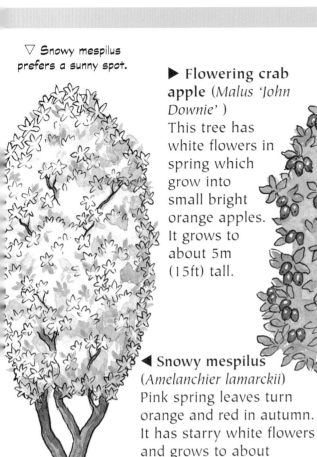

▽ Snowy mespilus prefers a sunny spot.

▶ **Flowering crab apple** (*Malus 'John Downie'*) This tree has white flowers in spring which grow into small bright orange apples. It grows to about 5m (15ft) tall.

◀ **Snowy mespilus** (*Amelanchier lamarckii*) Pink spring leaves turn orange and red in autumn. It has starry white flowers and grows to about 5m (15ft) tall.

▶ **Young's weeping birch** (*Betula pendula 'Youngii'*) This tree has silvery bark, small catkins in spring and golden-yellow leaves in autumn. Its slim branches droop – 'pendula' means hanging. It can reach 6m (18ft).

Beneath the boughs

Most plants don't like living under trees. Trees drink lots of water and create shade. But here are some that thrive. They should all be planted in autumn or spring, when the trees are leafless and the ground is moist. Add manure or compost to the planting holes. Cover the soil with bark, manure or leaf-mould to stop it drying out. Make a dip in the soil around the plants to catch rainwater.

◁ Evergreen periwinkle (*Vinca minor*) A tough little plant that hugs the ground and spreads quickly.

▽ Elephant's ears (*Bergenia cordifolia*) These have pink or red flowers in spring and evergreen glossy leaves.

▷ Rose of Sharon (*Hypericum calycinum*) An evergreen plant with golden flowers from early summer onwards.

▷ Bugle (*Ajuga reptans*) This spreads to make a carpet. It has long runners with baby plants all along.

Reach for the sky

All plants grow towards the light and have to jostle for space. Since climbers grow up rather than out, they take up less space and are great for small gardens.

Ways to climb

Twining stems wrap around any support available. Some go clockwise, others anti-clockwise.

Sweet peas ▷

◁ Tendrils are little, coiling outgrowths which clasp anything they find. Climbers like this are very skilful.

Twining leaf stalks cling like tendrils. After a few months they harden and are very hard to shift.

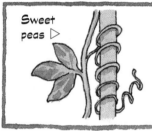

◁ Aerial roots need a rough surface, such as a brick wall or wooden fence, which they stick to like glue.

Thorns hook on and help plants to climb, but they need help. The stems must be tied to wires or trellis.

▶ **Honeysuckle**
(*Lonicera periclymenum*)
Type: twining stems.
How to grow: plant in autumn or spring.
Support: wires for trellis. Tie in the first shoots.
Height: up to 6m (18ft).
Flowers: in summer. Wonderful sweet scent.
Varieties: two of the best are Early Dutch (flowers in early summer and again in early autumn), and Late Dutch (flowers from mid-summer to autumn).

◀ **Clematis**
Type: twining leaf stalk.
How to grow: plant 10cm (4in) below the soil, to protect against a disease called wilt. This can kill off the top growth. Many clematis prefer light shade. Water if dry.
Support: will climb trellis, wires or a chain-link fence without help.
Height: up to 6m (18ft).
Flowers: many colours in all seasons.

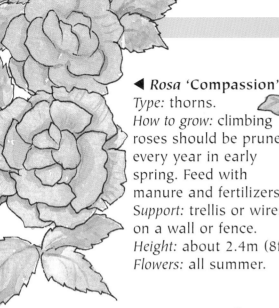

◄ *Rosa* 'Compassion'
Type: thorns.
How to grow: climbing roses should be pruned every year in early spring. Feed with manure and fertilizers.
Support: trellis or wires on a wall or fence.
Height: about 2.4m (8ft).
Flowers: all summer.

◄ **Climbing hydrangea**
(*Hydrangea petiolaris*)
Type: aerial roots.
How to grow: the perfect plant for a shady spot.
Support: wall or fence.
Height: up to 15m (45ft).
Flowers: in early summer.

▶ **Black-eyed Susan**
(*Thunbergia alata*)
Type: twining stems.
How to grow: plant seeds each year indoors in spring.
Support: canes.
Height: about 1.5m (4ft 6in).
Flowers: in summer.

▶ **Ivy**
(*Hedera*)
Type: aerial roots.
How to grow: ivy grows almost anywhere.
Support: wall.
Height: up to 24m (50ft) tall!
Flowers: ivy is grown for its many types of evergreen leaves.

Types of support

CHAIN-LINK FENCE

This can look bare and uninteresting, but is transformed with a whole host of climbing plants.

WALL AND FENCES

Aerial roots climb up these on their own. Twining stems or tendrils need wires, netting or trellis, too.

OLD TREE STUMPS

Plant honeysuckle or a climbing rose to grow over a stump for an attractive feature.

CONTAINERS

Use big pots, as the roots need to spread. Water well in dry weather.

Scents and smells

Lots of plants smell. Smelly leaves can put off grazing animals, or keep insects away. Flowers usually smell to attract insects. Sweet scents attract bees looking for nectar to make honey.

Outdoor scents

▲ **Damask rose** (*Rosa damascena*)
This flower has a lovely scent and is used in perfume.

◄ **Moss rose** (*Rosa centifolia 'Muscosa'*)
All green parts of this rose are covered with moss-like bristles. Its flowers are sweet smelling.

▲ **Lilac** (*Syringa*)
Sweet-scented lilac bushes flower in early summer.

▲ **Garden pinks** (*Dianthus plumarius*)
Garden pinks have been grown in gardens since the 1500s and have flowers that smell of cloves.

► **Regal lily** (*Lilium regale*)
The best lily to grow for scent. It has a strong, rich perfume.

Indoor smells

▲ **Jasmine** (*Jasminum polyanthum*)
A strong climber that has wonderful fragrant flowers from late spring onwards.

▲ **Lemon scented geranium** (*Pelargonium crispum*)
The leaves release a strong perfume in the sun, or when they are touched.

Winter scents

Fragrant honeysuckle (*Lonicera fragrantissima*) is an outdoor shrub that flowers in late winter. Its cream-coloured flowers are followed by red berries in spring.

Some indoor bulbs, such as hyacinths and daffodils (try 'Paper White'), smell gorgeous in the winter.

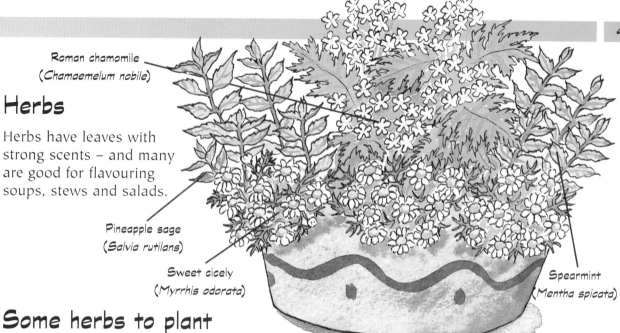

Roman chamomile
(*Chamaemelum nobile*)

Herbs

Herbs have leaves with strong scents – and many are good for flavouring soups, stews and salads.

Pineapple sage
(*Salvia rutilans*)

Sweet cicely
(*Myrrhis odorata*)

Spearmint
(*Mentha spicata*)

Some herbs to plant

Sweet cicely has small white flowers and leaves that have a pleasant sugary, aniseed flavour. You can chew them raw!

Pineapple sage can easily be grown from cuttings. If you rub the leaves they will give off a wonderful smell of pineapples.

Spearmint is the best mint for mint sauce or mint tea. Since mint will take over a garden if it can, plant in its pot.

Roman chamomile has scented leaves and daisy flowers. Pour boiling water on fresh or dried flower heads to make tea.

Planting a herb pot

▽ Make sure you get the right compost.

▽ See which arrangement looks best before you plant.

Herbs like well-drained soil. Take a pot with open holes in the bottom. Then add a layer of pebbles or broken clay pots.

Fill the pot to within 15cm (6in) of the top with soil-based (not peat-based) compost (ask for help at a garden centre).

Take the plants out of their pots (except mint, which would take over the whole pot if it was allowed to) and plant in the compost.

Meat-eating monsters?

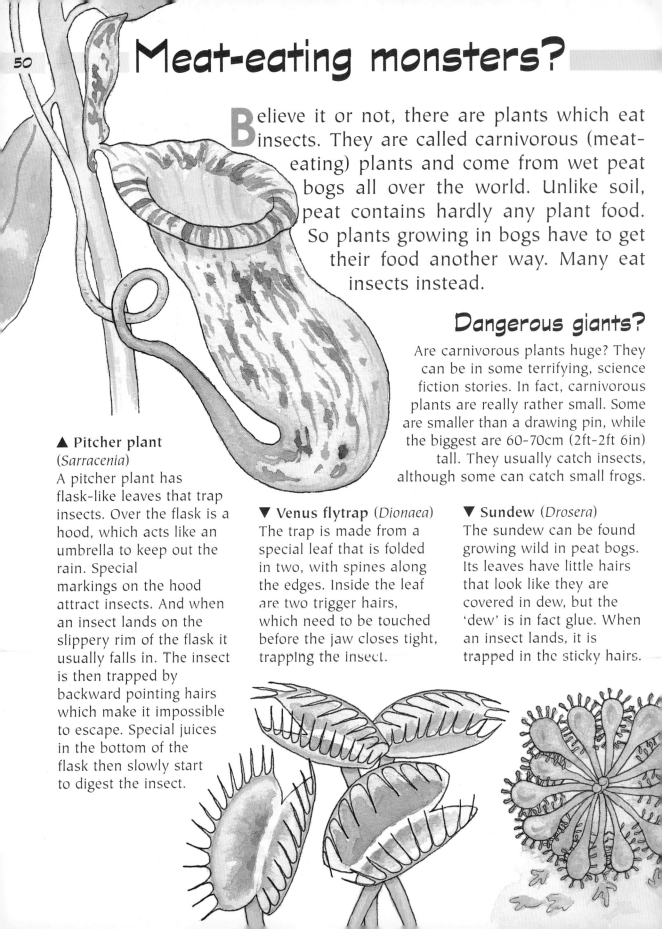

Believe it or not, there are plants which eat insects. They are called carnivorous (meat-eating) plants and come from wet peat bogs all over the world. Unlike soil, peat contains hardly any plant food. So plants growing in bogs have to get their food another way. Many eat insects instead.

Dangerous giants?

Are carnivorous plants huge? They can be in some terrifying, science fiction stories. In fact, carnivorous plants are really rather small. Some are smaller than a drawing pin, while the biggest are 60-70cm (2ft-2ft 6in) tall. They usually catch insects, although some can catch small frogs.

▲ Pitcher plant
(*Sarracenia*)
A pitcher plant has flask-like leaves that trap insects. Over the flask is a hood, which acts like an umbrella to keep out the rain. Special markings on the hood attract insects. And when an insect lands on the slippery rim of the flask it usually falls in. The insect is then trapped by backward pointing hairs which make it impossible to escape. Special juices in the bottom of the flask then slowly start to digest the insect.

▼ Venus flytrap (*Dionaea*)
The trap is made from a special leaf that is folded in two, with spines along the edges. Inside the leaf are two trigger hairs, which need to be touched before the jaw closes tight, trapping the insect.

▼ Sundew (*Drosera*)
The sundew can be found growing wild in peat bogs. Its leaves have little hairs that look like they are covered in dew, but the 'dew' is in fact glue. When an insect lands, it is trapped in the sticky hairs.

Caring for meat-eaters

Choose plants that look healthy, with new leaves growing at the bottom.

These plants are often sold in small pots to make them look bigger. If you buy one, find a slightly bigger pot.

Plants in danger

These amazing carnivorous plants have become very scarce in the wild. In the past, thousands were stripped from the swamps of America for sale as house plants. Also, when swampy land was drained for farming, the bogs where these plants lived dried out and the plants died.

◁ Take care not to damage the delicate roots.

◁ Use tap water only if it is boiled and cooled.

Should you buy them?

You may feel bad about buying one of these plants, but most are now raised in nurseries. A good garden centre will note on a label: 'Not taken from the wild.'

When you repot, you should always use peat as a compost because these plants grow in peat naturally.

Then stand the pot in a tray of rainwater that is 1-2cm ($\frac{1}{2}$-1in) deep, if you can.

About carnivorous plants

Carnivorous plants usually rest and lose their leaves in winter. Water them less, letting the tray dry out before refilling. Leave on a cool window sill or in a greenhouse. Your plants will grow again in spring. Should you feed them? You can, but they won't die if you forget, and it is easy to overfeed.

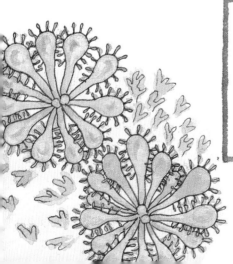

Tasty vegetables

Vegetables fresh from the garden are one of the great rewards of gardening. They are much tastier than bought ones, and packed full of vitamins, too. You can even grow small varieties in containers.

New potatoes

▽ Cover with compost so the pot is half full.

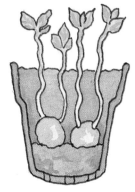

In spring, fill a large pot one-third full of potting compost. The bottom must have holes for drainage.

Put in two or three seed potatoes (you buy these from a garden centre), with the shoots pointing upwards.

Water well, then put the pot in a sheltered place outside where it will not catch the frost.

When the shoots are about 15cm (6in) tall, fill the pot up with compost. Yummy nutty potatoes will be ready in 10 to 12 weeks.

Tomatoes

△ Try small, cherry tomato varieties, such as 'Gardener's Delight' and 'Sweet 100'.

◁ Push a bamboo cane in behind each plant.

◁ One straight stem will produce better tomatoes.

In early summer, buy small plants. Put one in a pot at least 25cm (10in) wide, or two in a grow-bag (from a garden centre).

As the stem grows, tie it to the cane. Pull off side shoots growing between the leaf stems and the main stem.

Feed the plants with liquid seaweed or a special tomato feed once a week from early summer onwards.

◁ 'Lollo Rosso' has deep-red, frilled leaves.

△ 'Webb's Wonderful' is large with a heart of crispy-white leaves.

Lettuce

◁ Eat the small ones you pick.

Sow seed from early spring to early summer. Sow in short rows, 1cm (½in) deep and about 1cm (½in) apart.

After the seedlings have germinated, thin them out to leave about 15cm (6in) between each plant.

When they have grown into small lettuces, harvest every other one, leaving the rest plenty of room to grow.

◁ 'Little Gem' is small and tasty.

French beans

Plant seeds in pairs 15cm (6in) apart and 5cm (2in) deep, in early summer. If both germinate cut the top off the weaker one.

Radishes

You can start sowing radishes in early spring and continue until late summer. If you sow them at different times, they will ripen in turn. Sow the seed thinly 1-2cm (½-1in) deep, in rows about 10cm (4in) apart.

▷ French beans are ideal for containers. There are dwarf types 15-20cm (6-9in) tall, and climbing ones up to 1.8m (6ft) tall.

△ French beans cannot bear even a hint of frost.

◁ Eat whole when young, or slice when bigger.

The bean pods will grow to be 8-15cm (3-6in) long, and hang beneath the leaves. Pick them between 10 and 12 weeks after sowing.

▷ Radishes can take only three weeks from sowing to eating.

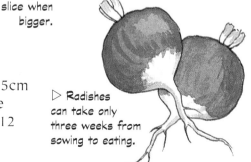

Fruit file

Some fruit plants, such as apple, pear and plum trees, take a while to grow and make fruit. But here are some you can enjoy more quickly.

Strawberries

Strawberries grow well in gardens or pots. Buy plants from a garden centre in late summer or early autumn, then plant them (see right). Fully-grown plants have long stems – called runners – with baby plants along them. See how to pot them up below.

▽ Make sure that the crown is just level with the soil.

◁ Crown

◁ Fruit start to grow in early summer.

△ Use soil improved with manure or compost. Space plants 30cm (12in) apart in the garden and at least 15cm (6in) apart in pots.

△ Strawberries are greedy plants. Feed them occasionally with fertilizers and water plants well in dry weather.

◁ Pick fruit when it turns bright red.

△ As the sunshine ripens the strawberries, pull any surrounding weeds out carefully to make sure the plants don't get smothered.

△ When no more new fruit grows, cut off all the old leaves at the base of the plant. Now new leaves will grow for next year's crop.

Runners

▷ The hook holds the runner against the soil.

▷ The baby will have fruit the next year.

Fill a small pot with garden soil. Choose the biggest baby plant on a strong strawberry runner.

Push a tent peg in beside the baby plant, so it comes out through a hole in the bottom.

Then push the peg into the soil next to the mother plant to hold the small pot firmly in place.

In a few weeks, the baby will have grown its own roots. Now you can cut the runner and plant it.

Blackcurrants

Delicious, juicy blackcurrant berries are great for pies, puddings and fruit drinks. By far the best one to grow is called 'Ben Sarek', a small variety that is perfect for growing in back gardens.

Plant a blackcurrant bush as you would a shrub (see page 38). After planting, add a mulch of manure to feed the bush and keep the soil moist. Once a year, give it a handful of fertilizer.

Every few years blackcurrant bushes need pruning. Simply cut about one third of the older stems right down to the ground. This allows new wood and a new crop of fruit to grow.

◁ 'Ben Sarek' grows about 1m (3ft) tall and makes very large berries.

Plants from pips

You can get lovely plants for free if you plant the pips of fruit. Just push the seed about 1cm (½in) deep into a small pot of compost. Some plants will have to be kept indoors because they come from hot places, but all make pretty plants to keep.

▷ Citrus trees can stay outside for most of the year, and just come in for the worst winter weather.

Grapevines grow from grape pips. They are climbing plants and make pretty house-plants while they are small. You can plant them outside when they get too big. They were even grown by the ancient Egyptians about 5,000 years ago!

You can plant any peanut as long as it hasn't been roasted, which kills the seeds. Crack each one across the middle to let moisture in and then plant several to one pot. They grow very quickly.

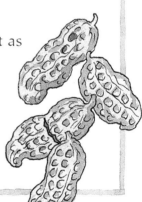

▷ Grow peanuts indoors or outside, in as much sun as possible.

Hanging baskets

A hanging basket is the perfect way to brighten up a dull corner or wall, and also is a great way to grow a collection of plants if you only have a little space. Baskets should be planted in spring or early summer after all danger of frost has passed. You can buy a basket and plants from a garden centre.

Planting a hanging basket

▽ Place the basket on a large plant pot or bucket to hold it firm while you work.

Water all the plants that will be put in the basket thoroughly and then leave them to drain.

▽ You may be able to rake up some moss from the lawn.

Line the basket with moss. If you don't have moss, use hay, or buy lining material from a garden centre.

▷ Use plastic taken from a carrier bag to help keep water in the basket and keep the compost moist.

Cut out a circle of plastic and lay on top of the moss. Fill the basket three-quarters full with potting compost.

▷ The roots should rest on the compost.

Now push small trailing plants through the sides of the basket. First wrap a plant tightly in newspaper. Push it out from inside the basket, leaves first.

▽ The newspaper protects the leaves as you pull plants through the mesh.

Hold the roots in place and pull the newspaper off through the mesh. Repeat around the basket with the other plants. They will grow to cover the sides.

▷ Leaving a 5cm (2in) gap between the rim of the basket and the compost allows room for watering.

Fill the basket nearly full with compost. Then plant an upright plant in the top such as a geranium or fuchsia. Gently firm down all the compost.

Plants for baskets

Warning!

Hanging baskets are very heavy once they are watered, so they must be hung from very strong hooks. Ask an adult to help you hang one up.

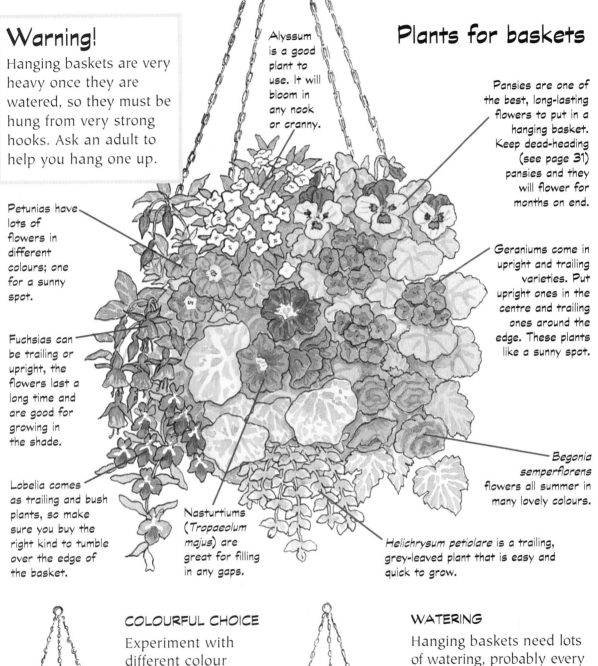

Alyssum is a good plant to use. It will bloom in any nook or cranny.

Pansies are one of the best, long-lasting flowers to put in a hanging basket. Keep dead-heading (see page 31) pansies and they will flower for months on end.

Petunias have lots of flowers in different colours; one for a sunny spot.

Geraniums come in upright and trailing varieties. Put upright ones in the centre and trailing ones around the edge. These plants like a sunny spot.

Fuchsias can be trailing or upright, the flowers last a long time and are good for growing in the shade.

Begonia semperflorens flowers all summer in many lovely colours.

Lobelia comes as trailing and bush plants, so make sure you buy the right kind to tumble over the edge of the basket.

Nasturtiums (*Tropaeolum majus*) are great for filling in any gaps.

Helichrysum petiolare is a trailing, grey-leaved plant that is easy and quick to grow.

COLOURFUL CHOICE

Experiment with different colour schemes. Plant a hanging basket with blue, white and grey plants for a cool scheme. Red, orange and yellow flowers gives a hot display.

WATERING

Hanging baskets need lots of watering, probably every day in the summer. They also need feeding at least once a week with a plant food made specially for flowers.

Wildlife in the garden

A garden is much more fun if you have wildlife visitors. Birds, butterflies, bees, and a whole range of interesting creatures will make your garden buzz with activity. But you will need to plan, make and plant special things to attract wildlife.

Make a loggery

Skylark ▷

The best time to get hold of logs is in autumn or winter. This is when tree surgeons are at work (they trim trees and cut off dangerous branches – you'll recognize them by their hard hats, climbing gear and chain saws). Ask if you can have some logs to make a loggery – the tree surgeons will be pleased to get rid of them. Or collect logs on country walks.

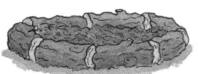

Make a ring of logs, burying each about 5cm (2in) deep. Put the most interesting sides facing out.

Fill the ring with leaves, compost and soil. Firm it in well. Add a smaller ring of logs on top. Fill this in, too.

Continue with another one or two layers until you are satisfied with the overall shape and design.

Planting

▽ Make a loggery in a slightly shady part of the garden.

Plant your loggery with woodland plants such as primroses, snowdrops, dwarf daffodils, crocuses, wood anemones, lily of the valley, ferns, ivy, dwarf campanula, bugle and forget-me-nots. Fill in around the plants with bulbs. For the finishing touch, cover with a layer of wood chips.

What's on the menu?

The food you put out will affect which birds visit:
Sunflower seeds, **corn** or a **peanut feeder** are liked by
house sparrows, doves, linnets, magpies, finches and tits.
A **fatty feeder** (see right) is good for insect eaters with
pointed bills, such as robins.
Grated cheddar cheese is a robin's favourite food.
Apple cores (left on the lawn) will be eaten by
blackbirds, starlings, magpies, and redwings.
Bread is OK, but it isn't the healthiest
food for birds.
Water should always be provided
in a shallow bowl. Birds need
it to drink and help fluff out
their feathers.

△ Starling

▷ Place the bird table
where you can easily see
it from a window.

△ House sparrow

△ Blue tit

△ Collared dove

◁ Make a bird table at
least 1.5m (4ft 6in) high
to be safe from cats.

▽ Cats are a menace
to bird tables. Place
table at least
2m (6ft) from
trees or shrubs
where cats could
hide to pounce
on birds.

When to feed

Once you have regular bird
visitors, keep the food supply
going or they will stop coming.
Ask a friend to feed the birds
if you have to go away.

Stop feeding birds in the
spring, as they can find plenty
of their natural foods and this
is best for their young
chicks. Start to feed
again in late autumn.

How to make a fatty feeder

Pierce a hole in the bottom
of a yogurt pot. Thread
through a piece of string.

String should be about
30cm (12in) long. ▷

Tie a small twig to the
string coming out of the
open end of the pot.

▷ Pull string so twig
rests against open end.

Melt some lard in a pan.
Stir in peanuts, dried fruit,
and seeds. Spoon carefully
into the yogurt pot.

Chaffinch ▷

◁ Sparrow

Cool in the fridge until the
mixture is hard. Pull off the
pot and hang feeder outside.

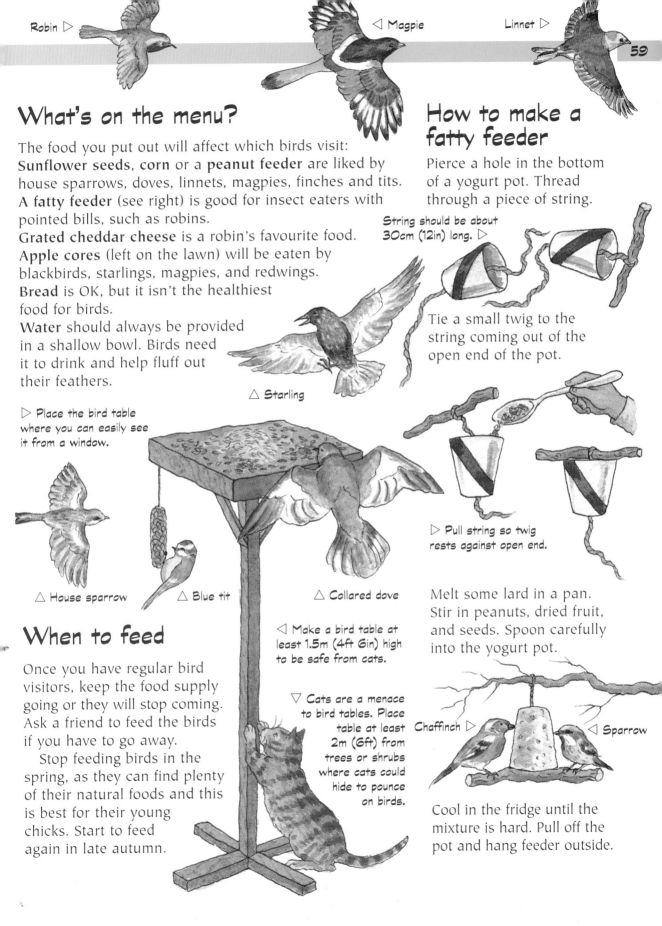

Butterflies and bees

Once you start growing flowers, butterflies and bees will find their own way into your garden. Encourage them to stay by growing some of their favourite plants. Many butterflies are becoming rare as new roads and buildings cover butterfly habitats, so you can be a friend to these delicate and beautiful creatures by giving them a place to feed and live.

△ Peacock

Butterfly border

Adult butterflies, and other insects such as hoverflies and bees, feed on the sugar-rich nectar of flowers. If you plant some of the flowers shown below, you'll give them plenty to eat throughout the summer season. Butterflies love sunshine, so grow your border in a sunny spot if you can.

Fragile life

The lifespan of a butterfly depends on its type and the climate. Some may live for only one week, just long enough to mate and lay eggs, while others may live for up to 10 months if they sleep during the winter.

△ Large white

Painted lady △

◁ Meadow brown

◁ Red admiral

EARLY SPRING
▽ Bugle
(*Ajuga reptans*)
is a spreading
plant with blue
flower spikes in
spring. It's a
popular early
plant with
butterflies and
grows in
shaded areas
under shrubs.

▽ *Viburnum tinus* 'Eve Price' is an evergreen shrub, flowering in winter and early spring.

▽ Primroses (*Primula vulgaris*) are good flowers for attracting several early butterflies.

SPRING
▽ Butterflies like wallflowers (*Erysimum*), plants that flower in spring and are planted in autumn.

EARLY SUMMER
▽ Sweet William (*Dianthus barbatus*) flowers in early summer. Sow seeds indoors in summer and plant out in autumn.

▽ Hebe *albicans* is an evergreen shrub with spikes of white that flowers from early summer onwards.

Bees

Bees are important to gardens. They pollinate flowers which then grow into fruit and seeds (see page 26). There are many kinds of bees. The best-known ones are honey bees and bumble bees. They both live in highly organised groups called colonies, or in hives.

Honey bees have very short lives that are filled with activity. Worker bees collect pollen and nectar from flowers and carry it back to the hive. Here the nectar is made into honey and is used with the pollen (which is rich in protein) to feed their larvae (babies). Bees also collect water from ponds and puddles, as well as resin from trees to make wax for their honeycombs, which is where they store honey in the hive.

Bumble bees have much thicker, hairier bodies than honey bees and their colonies are much smaller. If you look closely at them, you'll see that their bodies have many different colours and fascinating patterns.

▽ Bumblebee

Honey bee ▷

Beehive ▷

The pollen is carried in pollen baskets on the back legs. ▷

SUMMER
▽ There are lots of different kinds of lavender (*Lavandula*). All have beautifully scented flowers, usually in blue.

▽ Ice plant (*Sedum spectabile*). A perennial plant which comes up year after year and is much loved by butterflies. (See page 32.)

▽ Cornflowers (*Centaurea*) are easy to grow every year from seed. Sow straight into the flower bed in early autumn or spring.

▽ The flowers of the Butterfly bush (*Buddleia davidii*) are irresistible to many varieties of butterfly.

AUTUMN
▽ Michaelmas daisies (*Aster*), provide plenty of nectar for butterflies to stock up their energy before they sleep over the winter.

▽ Catmint (*Nepeta*) is one of many autumn flowering plants that attract butterflies. Others include: Lobelia, Honesty (*Lunaria*) and Ageratum.

Potted nature reserve

As more and more of the countryside gets eaten up by buildings, wildflowers and the insects that live on them are becoming rarer. But you can make a mini-wildlife reserve in your garden, or even in a pot, by planting wildflowers. You can buy wildflower seeds from most garden centres these days. They are easy to grow – just follow the instructions on the packet.

Sunny container

Plants from meadows, by the coast or mountains prefer lots of sun. Here are some good plants for a sunny container.

▽ Small scabious
(*Scabiosa columbaria*)

▽ Thrift
(*Armeria maritima*)

▷ Toadflax
(*Linaria vulgaris*)

▽ Corn marigold
(*Chrysanthemum segetum*)

Shady container

Plants that normally grow in woodland will grow well in shady corners. Here are some to try.

▽ Foxglove
(*Digitalis purpurea*)

▽ Primrose
(*Primula vulgaris*)

▽ Red campion
(*Silene dioica*)

▽ Ivy
(*Hedera helix*)

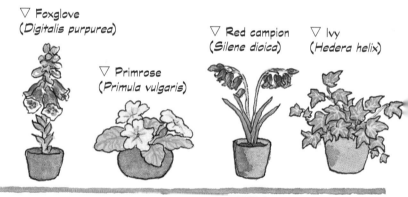

Boggy container

For once, use a container with no drainage holes for bog plants. These grow along the edges of streams or other boggy places and like to have damp roots.

▽ Lady's smock
(*Cardamine pratensis*)

▽ Marsh marigold
(*Caltha palustris*)

▽ Ragged robin
(*Lychnis flos-cuculi*)

▽ Monkey flower
(*Mimulus guttatus*)

Planting wildflowers

Wildflowers look best in containers made of natural materials. They must have drainage holes (except for a bog garden). Wildflowers grow best in compost with very little plant food in it, so seed compost is the best sort to use.

Choose plants according to whether the pot will be in the sun or shade. Some plants to try are shown here.

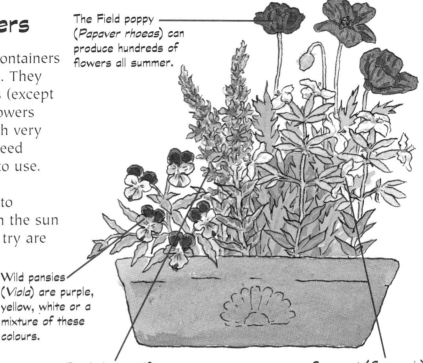

The Field poppy (*Papaver rhoeas*) can produce hundreds of flowers all summer.

Wild pansies (*Viola*) are purple, yellow, white or a mixture of these colours.

Purple loosestrife (*Lythrum*) is a tall plant with elegant flower spikes.

Soapwort (*Saponaria*) was once used for making soap!

Smaller pots look best if you plant just one kind of flower. Then group a few of these pots together for a pretty display.

Terracotta pots, wooden barrels, or stone troughs all make good containers for a wildflower garden. Grow a mixture of plants in a big pot.

Growing grasses

Ornamental grasses also grow well in containers, making interesting plants in their own right or creating a calming backdrop for more colourful flowers.

Hare's tail (*Lagurus*) is a dainty grass with silky, soft flowers.

Many animals and birds like to eat grains of Foxtail barley (*Hordeum*).

Making a mini-pond

Even a tiny pond will make a garden come alive. A mini-pond may not be large enough to provide a home for goldfish, but birds and insects will love it and you can grow one or two unusual water-loving plants.

Preparing a pond

▷ Air from the water will get into the basket, so the roots can breathe.

◁ The roots can grow through the sides.

You need a big, watertight container. Use half an old wooden barrel lined with plastic, or a plastic toy tidy.

Fill the bottom with about 5cm (2in) of gravel, then fill with water. Use rainwater if you can, or tap water.

There is no soil in the pond, so use a special net basket. You can buy one from a garden centre.

▽ The pots rest on the bottom.

Zebra rushes

Put garden soil in the baskets and firm plants in so they can't float away. Top up with gravel.

Lower the pots gently into place around the edge of the pond. A half-barrel will hold five or six plants.

Waterlilies

Plants to grow

King cup (*Caltha palustris*)
This is the first aquatic plant to bloom in the spring, with masses of golden-yellow flowers.

Waterlilies (*Nymphaea*)
Most waterlilies grow too large for a mini-pond, but some dwarf ones, such as *Nymphaea pygmaea* will grow in a large container.

Zebra rush (*Scirpus zebrinus*)
A striking plant with straight stems banded in green and white.

▲ **Water forget-me-not**
(*Myosotis scorpioides*)
Bright blue flowers with yellow or pink eyes make this plant very pretty. It even grows in the shade.

Plants for oxygen

Plants called oxygenating plants release oxygen for pond animals to breathe and help keep water clear.

△ Hornwort (*Ceratophyllum*)
This plant floats just below the surface of the water.

Oxygenating plants are usually sold in bunches, with a piece of lead to weigh them down in the water. Plant a bunch in a small pot of compost and lower it into the pond.

△ Canadian pond weed
(*Elodea canadensis*)
Roots and spreads easily, producing masses of stems.

Pea soup

After about a week the pond is likely to turn into pea soup. Don't panic! It is doing exactly what it should. It is simply a natural explosion of algae (minute water plants). They feed on all the minerals in the water. Once they have fed, the water will go clear again.

Pond care

The small amount of water in your mini-pond can evaporate (dry up) or freeze quickly. If you have a garden, dig a hole to sink the pond into. This will keep the temperature more even. If not, top up every so often with water. Remove dead leaves and keep plants pruned if they grow too large.

King cups

Houseplants

ouseplants are plants that you grow in your home or in a greenhouse, usually because they are too delicate to survive outdoors all year round in cool climates. They are sometimes called exotic plants, which just means that they come from another country, although 'exotic' can also mean strange and unusual-looking.

Cruelty to houseplants

Just like any plants, houseplants need light, soil and water. Many houseplants are easy to keep, and can cope with varied conditions. Some are fussier and may die slowly unless you know how to treat them. Sadly, some people who sell houseplants don't take much care of them in their shop, or give advice on how to look after them – after all, if it dies, you can buy a new one. But it is sad to see a plant neglected and dying when just a little care can turn it into a lush plant worthy of the name 'exotic'.

In the house

Don't put houseplants in a dark corner. Some places may seem light to you, but compared with the light outside, even on a grey day, they may be much too dark for a plant.

◁ Houseplants which have red or purple undersides to their leaves prefer more shaded places.

Many houseplants don't like a dry atmosphere, such as being too near a radiator. The plant will get dry, brown patches on its leaves.

◁ Generally, the lighter green the leaves, the closer to the window the plant should be.

Top tips for houseplants

To keep a plant moist, stand its pot on pebbles in a tray. Fill the tray with water (but not touching the bottom of the pot). The water evaporates slowly, making the air around the plant moist. Or you can spray the plant with a water sprayer several times a day.

Houseplant pests

Many houseplants can be attacked by pests or diseases. Check any new plants you bring into the house for unhealthy signs. If a plant starts to look poorly, even in good conditions, take a close look with a magnifying glass for tiny insects.

There are chemical sprays for pests which can be dangerous if they are not used properly. For a single plant – if there are not too many pests – it's best just to squash them between finger and thumb.

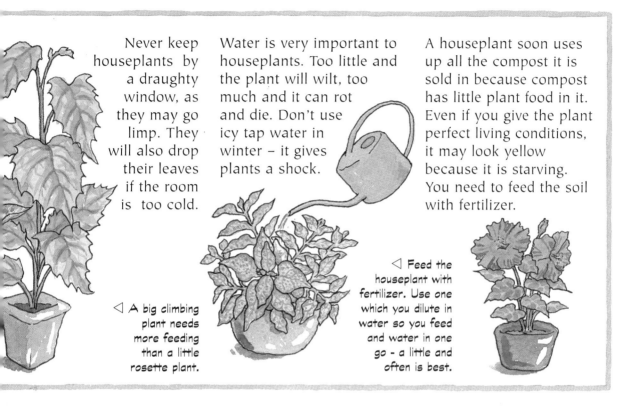

Never keep houseplants by a draughty window, as they may go limp. They will also drop their leaves if the room is too cold.

Water is very important to houseplants. Too little and the plant will wilt, too much and it can rot and die. Don't use icy tap water in winter – it gives plants a shock.

A houseplant soon uses up all the compost it is sold in because compost has little plant food in it. Even if you give the plant perfect living conditions, it may look yellow because it is starving. You need to feed the soil with fertilizer.

◁ A big climbing plant needs more feeding than a little rosette plant.

◁ Feed the houseplant with fertilizer. Use one which you dilute in water so you feed and water in one go - a little and often is best.

A history of houseplants

In the 1900s, and up to around fifty years ago, most people's houses were not warm or light enough for exotic plants. Only rich people could build expensive glasshouses, heated by coal, to keep plants in.

It was considered a very smart hobby in the 1900s to grow the latest exotic plants, brought back from parts of the globe that were just being explored. A few people had marvellous collections. Nowadays, most people can grow houseplants in their homes if they want to and it's easy to forget how special these exotic plants were to our great-grandparents.

Take a closer look at your houseplants. Some are from the rainforest; some would be trees, if they had the space. On a single windowsill you may have plants from tropical places that are thousands of miles apart!

Some houseplants to grow

All these houseplants are easy to find. This is how you look after them.

BEGONIA

Origin: tropical forests all over the world.
Plant facts: There are nearly one thousand different types of begonia, which are mainly grown for their red, purple, green or silver-spotted leaves.
Care: allow begonias to dry between waterings, as they rot if they get too wet.
Conditions: begonias with colourful leaves go green in bright sunlight, so grow these plants in a slightly shaded place.

▽ Feed begonias regularly in the growing season, avoiding getting plant food on their leaves.

AFRICAN VIOLETS (Saintpaulia)

Origin: Central Africa.
Plant facts: these plants have furry leaves and lots of flowers, usually in shades of purple or pink.
Care: over-watering will kill off African violets, so never let the compost get soggy. Feed every two weeks in the growing season. Keep water off the leaves as in bright sun, water drops magnify the sun's rays and burn them.
Conditions: African violets grow best in shadier, north-facing parts of the house.

▽ Letting African violets dry out a little between waterings will encourage more flowers to grow.

FIGS (Ficus)

Origin: India.
Plant facts: there are many types of figs; Fiddle leaf fig, Weeping fig and the Rubber plant.
Care: figs often grow into huge trees in the wild, but will stay small if you keep them in small pots - the bigger the pot, the bigger the plant.
Conditions: all figs like much the same conditions – a light spot, well away from cold draughts.

▷ Give a fig pot a quarter-turn each day to stop it leaning into the light and getting lop-sided.

HIPPEASTRUM

Origin: South America.
Plant facts: These are the most impressive flowering bulbs ever. Flower stalks sometimes reach 90cm (3ft) tall, producing lily-like flowers.
Care: choose a pot that allows 2.5cm (1in) of space between the bulb and the edge of the pot. Plant the bulb so that one-third shows above the compost. Feed regularly.
Conditions: Keep this plant in warm, light conditions.

▽ Water hippeastrum once or twice a week during winter and spring, more often in summer.

CYCLAMEN

Origin: dry, Mediterranean countries.
Plant facts: the cyclamen has bright flowers with swept back petals. A very popular winter-flowering houseplant.
Care: after flowering, a plant will carry on growing until late spring. When no new buds are showing, stop watering, so that the leaves turn yellow and die. Leave it dry all summer. Towards late summer, the plant will show signs of growth, which is the signal to start watering again.
Conditions: Grow in a cool, bright room.

▽ Cyclamen bloom throughout the winter.

PEACE LILY (*Spathiphyllum*)

Origin: South America.
Plant facts: This plant has white spathe flower bracts (these are like special leaves around the flower). In the wild, some species actually grow underwater!
Care: it's hard to overwater this plant, but be very careful not to let it dry out. After flowering, the spathe will turn green, so cut it back to the base.
Conditions: peace lilies will grow in darker rooms where their white flower bracts will show up well.

▽ The leaves last a long time, so keep them dusted.

Making more houseplants

You can get new plants from cuttings of houseplants, just like from garden plants. This is a great way to grow baby plants to put in pots and give as gifts.

GERANIUM (*Pelargonium*)

Cut off the top 7.5cm (3in) from a long stem. Trim the bottom leaves.

Make a hole next to the mother plant with a stick, then push the cutting in.

After a few weeks, dig the cutting up with a dibber. If it has grown roots, plant in its own pot of compost.

▷ If there are no roots, try again with another stem.

SPIDER PLANT (*Chlorophytum comosum*)

Spider plants grow stems with baby plants on the end.

Snip the babies off the stem and plant in small pots of compost.

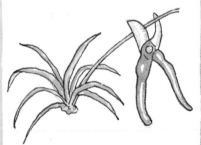

The small plants take root easily and will soon start to grow.

PRAYER PLANT (*Maranta*)

This plant gets its name from its habit of folding its leaves at night.

In spring, a large plant can be taken out of its pot and split into several pieces.

Plant the pieces in separate pots. They will soon make new plants.

Houseplant display

A windowsill can soon become overcrowded with plants and you will have to find new places for them. Plant pots can ruin good furniture, so make use of wooden crates instead (try and get some from a greengrocer).

Growing on trees in tropical forests, the urn plant (*Bromeliad*) absorbs water through its leaves, not its roots. So keep urn leaves topped up with water.

Christmas cacti (*Schlumbergera*) are succulents (see page 74). They produce one bright pink flower at the end of each stem - usually just before Christmas!

Mother-in-law's tongue (*Sansevieria*) is grown for its long, sword-like leaves. It doesn't need much water.

Make your display high enough to catch plenty of light from the window.

There are many types of flowering begonias, which will add colour to your display.

The Piggyback plant (*Tolmiea*) produces baby plants on top of older leaves.

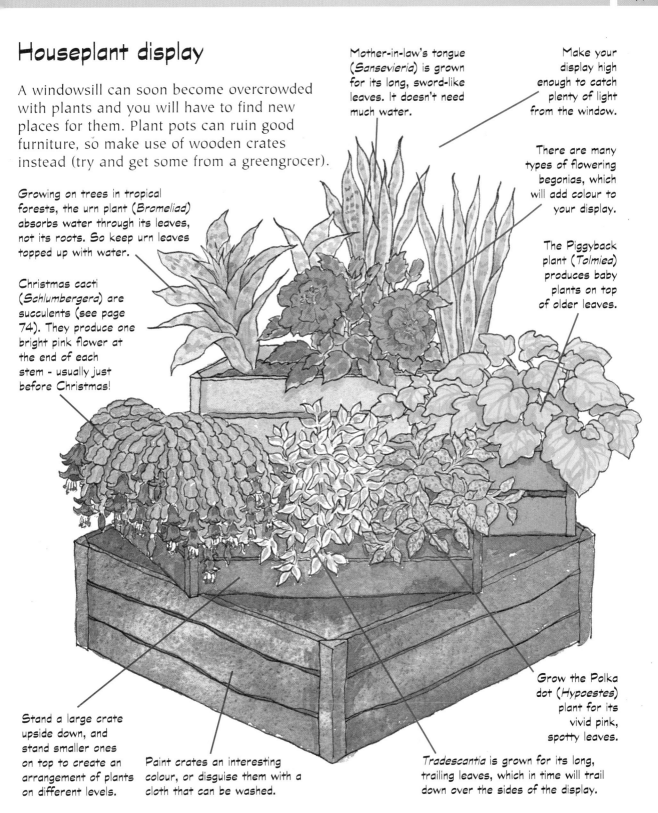

Stand a large crate upside down, and stand smaller ones on top to create an arrangement of plants on different levels.

Paint crates an interesting colour, or disguise them with a cloth that can be washed.

Tradescantia is grown for its long, trailing leaves, which in time will trail down over the sides of the display.

Grow the Polka dot (*Hypoestes*) plant for its vivid pink, spotty leaves.

Cacti and succulents

Cacti are very popular houseplants. They come from desert areas of the world and live in the driest conditions. But this doesn't mean they will put up with neglect and survive as dusty specimens that hardly grow at all. With just a little care and attention they will grow well and produce fabulous flowers every year.

Spines grow along the ridges of the stem. They help to shade the plant.

Some spines trap warm air during the day to protect the cactus from extreme cold at night.

◀ Goldfinger cactus (*Notocactus leninghausii*) These are quite greedy plants, so feed them regularly in spring and summer. They have large yellow flowers.

What's a succulent?

Succulents are plants with thick, fleshy stems or leaves, which can store water for the plant to use during long, hot summers. All cacti are succulents, but not all succulents are cacti – there are other species of succulent plants, too.

About spines

True cacti have fleshy stems, but no leaves. They usually have spines instead. The spines of the cactus are, in fact, leaves, but instead of being wide and flat, they have become thin and needle-like. Water evaporates easily from flat leaves, but spines only have a small surface for water to escape from. Because the spines aren't green, they can't make energy for the plant like normal leaves do (see page 11). But the stem of the cactus is green so it can do the job instead.

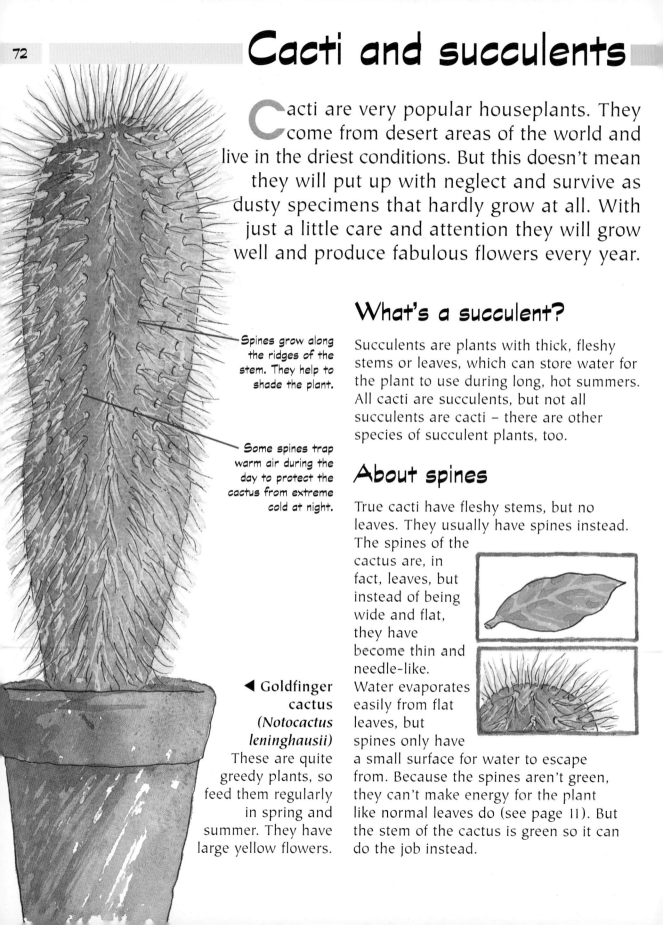

Caring for cacti

▽ Cacti soil must never get soggy.

Always buy special cactus compost, or use soil-based compost mixed half and half with sharp sand or grit.

During the winter, put cacti on a tray of gravel and only moisten the gravel if they shrivel.

In spring, cacti start to grow, so you need to start watering. Give plants just a little at first.

Do not re-pot cacti until roots grow out of the bottom of the pot. Move to a 1cm (½in) larger pot.

Take great care when handling cacti. Their spines and hairs can hurt you. Always wear gloves.

Before you move them, wrap several sheets of newspaper around the cactus, like this.

Some cacti and succulents to grow

Here and on the next page you can see some of the easiest succulent plants to grow.

▷ Rebutias are small round plants that flower easily. They have a wide range of flower colours.

▽ Pincushion cactus (*Mammillaria wildii*) This is a good plant for beginners as it's tough and fast-growing.

More about cacti

Taking cuttings

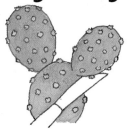

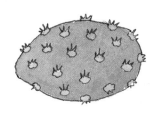

You can grow new cactus plants from cuttings. Take them in spring or early summer. Use a sharp knife to take off a side branch.

Leave the cutting until the cut surface has dried out. This may take a week or two, but if you don't do it, the cutting will rot.

Put the cutting into the same pot of compost as the mother plant. It will grow roots in a few weeks. Then move the baby into its own pot.

More plants to grow

▼ **Peanut cactus** (*Chamaecereus silvestrii*) A strong growing plant with bold flowers.

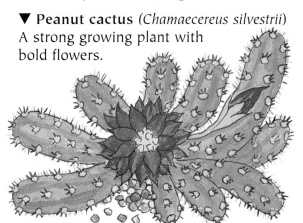

▶ **Golden barrel cactus** (*Echinocactus grusonii*) This grows into a large, rounded plant, with ribbed stems armed with sharp, yellow spines.

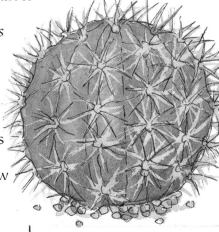

DESERT DISH GARDEN

Cacti and succulents can make a very attractive desert dish garden. Surround the plants with some interesting rocks.

◀ **Partridge breast** (*Aloe variegata*) A succulent plant from the African desert.

◄ Christmas cactus
(*Schlumbergera*)
Not all cacti come
from dry places. This
one comes from tropical
rainforests. It prefers shadier,
moister conditions than desert
cacti. For a good display of flowers,
leave the plant dry and cool for a
couple of months after flowering.
Then water regularly and put
outside in a shady spot for the
summer. In the autumn, flower
buds will form. Bring the plant
indoors for the flowers to open.

▷ Be very
careful. These
bristles are
extremely
difficult to
remove if
they get
onto your
skin.

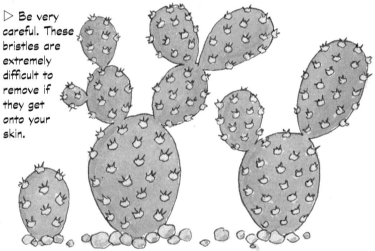

▲ Prickly pear cactus (*Opuntia*)
There are many types, but all have oval pads.
Grow new plants using the pads as cuttings.

► Jade plant
(*Crassula
argentea*)
A fine, strong-
growing plant
that eventually
grows into a
bush about 1m
(3ft) tall. It
makes an
attractive 'tree'
in a pot.

Cactus flowers

Many cacti have very bright
flowers. Red or orange flowers,
for instance, are often
pollinated by humming birds in
the wild.

Cacti must be kept cool in
winter for flower buds to form.
Modern central heating keeps
the house too warm. In autumn,
when you start to water less,
move the cactus to a much
cooler place. A cool hall,
porch or spare bedroom
(where the heating is turned
off) is fine. In spring, bring
the plant back into the
warm and start watering
and feeding it. You will
soon see flower buds!

Everlasting flowers

One way to enjoy flowers all year round is to dry them. It is simple to do, costs nothing and they make a great gift for a friend or relation. In spring and summer, there are lots of flowers to dry, and in autumn you can find seed-heads – try collecting and drying anything and everything!

△ Wild flowering grasses are a favourite - you will be amazed at how many different sorts there are. Collect them when you are out on summer walks in the country.

How to dry flowers

△ Coat-hangers make ideal drying racks. You can tie several bunches along the bottom.

Collect flowers on a sunny day, just before they are fully open. If the flowers have been open for a few days, then the petals will drop as they dry.

Remove some of the longer leaves, then tie several stems together. Arrange the flower heads at different levels so that they don't crush each other.

Hang the flowers upside down in a warm, airy room until they turn dry and crispy.

△ Strawflower (*Helichrysum*) and sea lavender (*Limonium*) are two good flowers to plant in spring, specially for drying. Sow the seeds in small pots and plant them in the garden when they are big enough.

△ Honesty (*Lunaria*) has seed pods that look like large silvery discs. That's how it got the nickname, 'Silver penny'. Honesty will grow almost anywhere, spreading its seeds around the garden to grow into new plants.

△ English lavender (*Lavendula*) has a wonderful smell that lasts for ages. Arrange it simply in a vase, or pull the dried flowers off the stalks and put them in little bowls to make rooms smell nice.

△ Roses should be cut for drying just as the flower bud is opening. They dry slowly, but keep their colour and perfume beautifully.

▷ Don't put water in the vase after you have arranged the flowers.

Then remove the rest of the leaves, tidy them up and make an arrangement in a vase.

△ Poppies (*Papaver*) have seed pods that are rather like natural salt and pepper pots because they shake the seeds out of holes at the top. These pods are very tough and can be painted in any colour (try gold or silver for Christmas).

△ Love-in-a-mist (*Nigella*) has charming flowers of soft blue, surrounded by a collar of ferny leaves.

But it is the handsome striped, papery seed pods that are mostly used in arrangements of dried flowers.

Plant first aid

◁ Aphids

Here you will find out about some of the most common pests and diseases that affect plants, how you can deal with them and which garden creatures will help keep pests at bay.

Garden enemies

▷ A hungry cabbage white caterpillar.

FLOWERS AND TREES

Aphids (greenfly)
Victims: aphids suck out the juices of many plants.
Symptoms: leaves curl up and buds or flowers become misshapen.
Treatment: wipe them off with a cloth or use a jet of water from a hose-pipe.

▽ Some insecticides can kill all the good insects, as well as the bad.

Leafscorch
Victims: many plants, also newly-planted trees.
Symptoms: edges of leaves turn brown, curl up and leaves can fall off.
Treatment: on hot, sunny days prevent leaf scorch by watering early in the day.

◁ Leaf scorch

Powdery mildew
Victims: many plants, particularly often roses.
Symptoms: a white or grey powdery coating appears on shoots and buds. Leaves curl up.
Treatment: avoid growing roses in shady places and make sure the stems are not overcrowded.

Slugs and snails
Victims: all young plants and seedlings.
Symptoms: holes eaten into the leaves.
Treatment: slugs and snails mainly feed at night, so collect them in a jar in the evening. Let them out in a field where they can't damage your plants.

VEGETABLES AND FRUIT

Cabbage white caterpillars
Victims: brussel sprouts, cabbages and cauliflowers. The cabbage white butterfly lays its eggs on these

vegetables. The eggs then hatch into caterpillars.
Symptoms: holes eaten into vegetable leaves.
Treatment: when you see holes in the leaves, pick the caterpillars off.

Codling moth
Victims: apples.
Symptoms: the maggot in your apple is the larva (baby) of a moth which lays its eggs on young apples. The eggs hatch into caterpillars that eat into the fruit.
Treatment: eat all apples carefully!

Spider mites
Victims: many houseplants.
Symptoms: the first sign of attack from tiny, sap-sucking spider mites is silvery speckles on the leaves.
Treatment: spray with a fine mist of water at least twice a day as spider mites hate wet feet.

Spider mites ▷

Garden friends

Most garden wildlife consists of useful, interesting creatures that feed on many of the 'baddy' insects. To help grow healthy plants, welcome them into your garden.

Ladybirds
Both spotted ladybirds and their larvae, feed on large numbers of greenfly.

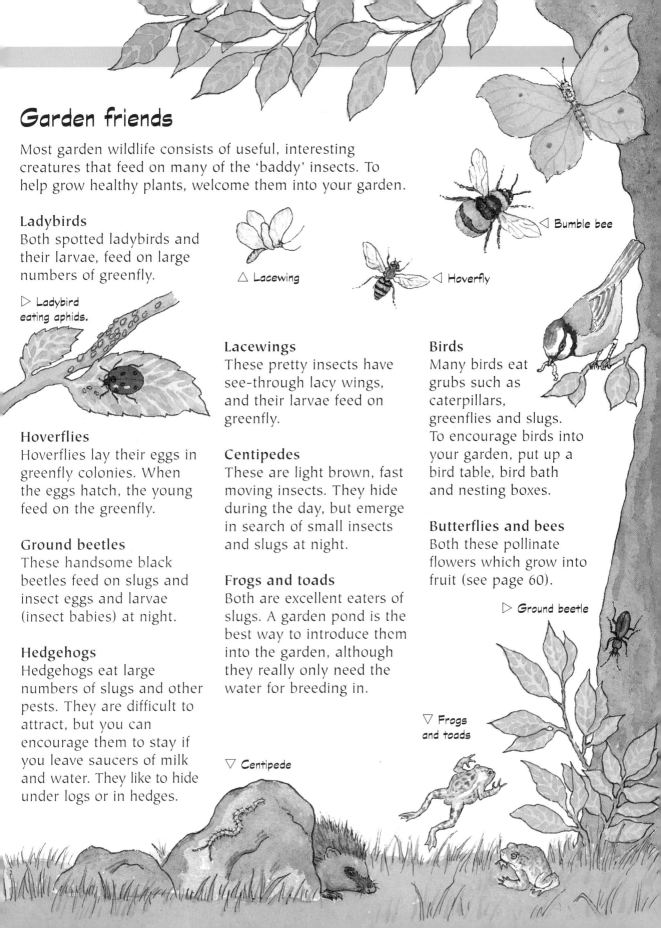

△ Lacewing

◁ Bumble bee

◁ Hoverfly

▷ Ladybird eating aphids.

Lacewings
These pretty insects have see-through lacy wings, and their larvae feed on greenfly.

Birds
Many birds eat grubs such as caterpillars, greenflies and slugs. To encourage birds into your garden, put up a bird table, bird bath and nesting boxes.

Hoverflies
Hoverflies lay their eggs in greenfly colonies. When the eggs hatch, the young feed on the greenfly.

Centipedes
These are light brown, fast moving insects. They hide during the day, but emerge in search of small insects and slugs at night.

Ground beetles
These handsome black beetles feed on slugs and insect eggs and larvae (insect babies) at night.

Frogs and toads
Both are excellent eaters of slugs. A garden pond is the best way to introduce them into the garden, although they really only need the water for breeding in.

Butterflies and bees
Both these pollinate flowers which grow into fruit (see page 60).

▷ Ground beetle

Hedgehogs
Hedgehogs eat large numbers of slugs and other pests. They are difficult to attract, but you can encourage them to stay if you leave saucers of milk and water. They like to hide under logs or in hedges.

▽ Frogs and toads

▽ Centipede

Through the seasons

A garden changes all year round. From spring, plants start to grow, putting out leaves, shoots and flowers. They grow until late autumn, then slow down for the winter. But there are always things to do.

Spring

Spring is the busiest season of the year for gardeners. Many seeds can be sown once the soil has warmed up. Looking at hedges will tell you if it is warm enough – when they begin to show green, it is time to start.

◆ Flowers to sow – straight in the soil or in a small pot – include annuals such as sunflowers, clarkia, cornflowers, love-in-a-mist and sweet peas.
◆ Vegetables, such as radishes, lettuces and tomatoes, can be sown outside. Plant early potatoes in pots, either indoors or outdoors.

◆ Sprinkle fertilizer around shrubs to feed them as they start to grow.
◆ Dig up old perennial plants, such as daisies delphiniums, and lupins, and divide them into several pieces using a spade. Replant and each piece will grow again.
◆ Clear weeds from flower-beds, then put on a mulch to stop weeds growing back again and to keep moisture in the soil.

◆ If you have a pond, top up pond plant baskets with soil, finishing with a gravel layer.

Indoors

• Sow seeds of half-hardy flowers such as marigolds, snapdragons and petunias. Sow in small pots and keep on a sunny windowsill.
• Dust houseplants down and increase watering. Start feeding houseplants regularly.
• Check the roots of houseplants by knocking them gently out of their pots. If the roots look all squashed up, then replant in a pot that is about 2.5cm (1in) bigger all round.

◁ Prune roses by cutting back long shoots by about two-thirds. Make clean, sloping cuts just above a bud, using a pair of secateurs.

▽ Plant summer flowering bulbs, such as gladioli.

Summer

Watering is one of the most important jobs to do in the garden in summer and should never be neglected.

◆ In early summer plant hanging baskets, window boxes and pots with summer flowers. Start to feed them with fertilizer after three or four weeks.
◆ Put in stakes to support tall growing plants such as sunflowers and delphiniums.
◆ Containers and hanging baskets will need watering at least once a day in the warm weather.
◆ Sow French and runner beans outside.
◆ Keep weeds under control by using a hoe to cut under the roots.

◆ Thin out flower and vegetable seedlings grown outside in spring.
◆ Prune early flowering shrubs, such as forsythia and flowering currants, thinning out old shoots.
◆ Sow wallflowers, foxgloves, sweet William and honesty which will all flower next year.
◆ Dead-head all flowers as they start to fade. This stops seeds forming and makes the plant produce more flowers.
◆ Feed all summer flowers regularly and plant in pots, containers or grow bags.
◆ Continue to sow lettuce and radish. Make a new

strawberry plant from the 'runners'.
◆ In long, hot spells concentrate on watering young trees and shrubs that were planted earlier in the year.
◆ In late summer, take cuttings of long-lived flowers, such as marguerites, fuchsias and geraniums.
◆ Sow hardy annuals outside in order to get early flowers next year.

◁ Keep pond weed under control by thinning it out a little every week or so.

Indoors

● Continue to water and feed houseplants regularly. To increase your collection, try taking some cuttings. Many houseplants root easily during the summer months.

Autumn

The beginning of autumn is the main harvesting season for fruit and vegetables. There is a chilly nip in the air and delicate plants should be brought indoors.

△ Cut off green tomatoes and leave to ripen on a sunny windowsill.

◆ Dig up geraniums and fuchsias. Put into small pots and take indoors or put in a shed. Keep these plants fairly dry over the winter. In early spring, start to water and watch them burst into growth. Replant in bigger pots.

◆ Plant bulbs as soon as possible.
◆ Clear away annual bedding plants such as petunias and marigolds. In their place, plant spring flowers, such as primroses wallflowers, foxgloves and forget-me-nots.

Indoors

• Stop feeding all your houseplants.
• Group houseplants together in a light spot away from radiators. Being in the company of other plants helps keep moist air around the leaves.
• Collect autumn leaves and make cards or pictures.

◆ For fresh herbs for the winter, plant a few pieces of root in a pot from mint plants and keep them on a windowsill indoors.

▽ Rake up leaves from lawns and flower-beds. Pile into a heap to make leaf mould.

◆ In early autumn take cuttings from shrubs. Put the tips of shoots 10-15cm (4-6in) long into pots of compost and bury them in the ground. Keep out the worst of the weather by covering them with the top of a plastic bottle.
◆ Put a net over the pond to stop leaves falling in.

Winter

It may be cold and wet outside, but on fine days there is plenty of tidying up to do in the garden. The more you do now, the easier it will be in the spring.

◆ Digging or walking on your soil when it's wet will damage it. If it sticks to your boots, keep off. On sunny days you can weed, dig or fork the soil and add compost or manure.

◆ Make any changes to shapes of flower beds.

◆ Plant trees and shrubs. They live for a long time, so find out how big they grow and plant them in a place with plenty of room.

◆ Make a compost bin out of bamboo canes and chicken wire. Recycled kitchen waste is great for the garden.

◆ Birds get hungry on cold winter days. Make some new friends this winter by putting out some food.

△ A hanging basket full of nuts will help the birds survive in winter.

△ To cheer up winter days, plant a container with winter-flowering heathers and pansies.

◁ Check tree ties to make sure they are not too tight. A length of old tights or stockings makes a good tree tie because it stretches as the tree grows and moves.

▷ A seed tray garden.

Thyme   Dwarf box   Mini-rose

Sisyrinchium brachypus

Moss as 'lawn'

Sempervivum

Indoors

• Houseplants kept on windowsills suffer when the temperature suddenly drops, so always bring them in from behind the curtain at night.

• Browse through seed catalogues to get ideas for next year.

• Make an indoor garden in a seed tray (see left) and become a landscape gardener in miniature.

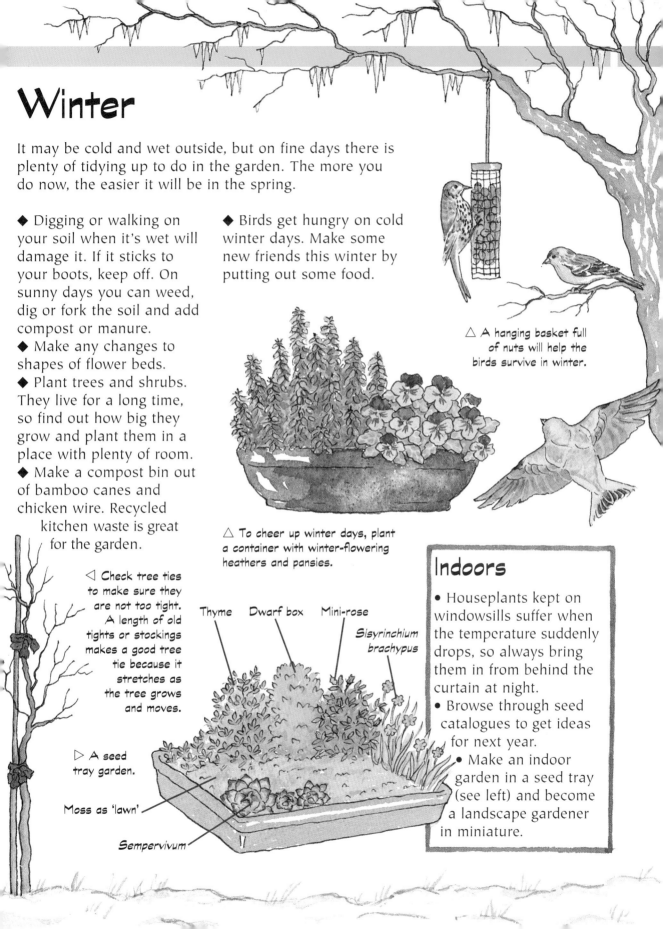

World of plants

Botanists reckon there are about 350,000 different types of plants in the world. They are sorted into groups, according to things they have in common; for example, what they look like, how they reproduce, their way of life, and so on. This is called classification.

Plant categories

Here are the eight main categories of plants recognised by botanists.

Algae live in all kinds of water.

Fungi have no chlorophyll (see page 11) and therefore are not green.

A **lichen** is a fungus combined with an alga (the singular of algae).

Mosses and **ferns** reproduce with spores instead of seeds.

Conifers are trees that have cones.

Flowering Plants

Many flowering plants have soft stems. **Climbers** have long twisting stems.

Shrubs are smaller, with woody stems.

Trees are usually large, with thick trunks of wood.

Plant names

Plants are mostly called by their common names – names such as poppy and marigold. These names were made up in the past by anybody. Flowers are called different things in different countries, and even inside one country the same flower can have different names, or sometimes two flowers can have the same name.

Botanists give plants Latin names, following strict rules, made up by the great Swedish botanist, Carolus Linnaeus. He first named thousands of plants in the 1700s and now new plants are always named according to his ordered system, which uses Latin names. This means gardeners everywhere in the world know exactly which plant they are talking about when they use the Latin name. You can tell all sorts of things about a plant from its proper, Latin name. Plant names are made up of two parts, rather like a person's first and second name.

◀ *Rhododendron campanulatum*: *rodo* means a rose, and *dendron*, a tree. *Campanulatum* means bell-shaped flowers.

▶ *Bellis perennis*: *Bellis* means pretty, and *perennis* a perennial (a plant that lives for many years).

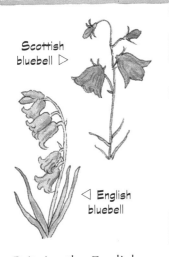

Scottish bluebell ▷

◁ English bluebell

In Britain, the English and Scottish both have a flower called a bluebell, but they are completely different plants.

◀ *Helianthus annuus*: *Helio* means sun, *anthos*, flower, and *annuus*, an annual (a plant which grows every year from seed, then dies).

Gifts from the garden

Flowers and plants of all kinds make wonderful gifts. You can just give the plant as it is, or try some of these clever ideas to present them. You'll also find out how to make some useful gifts for gardeners here.

Blooming baskets

▷ Choose plants that will last indoors for a few weeks, and can then be planted outside.

Buy a small wicker basket. Put three small plants in pots in it.

▷ Use a trailing plant such as ivy.

Fill up the basket with home-made plant labels (see right), and flower seeds you have collected.

Then add a label and dress the basket with ribbons, bows and fir cones. Your gift is now ready!

Plant labels

Cut down the side of a large yogurt pot. Then cut out the circular bottom and cut off the rim at the top.

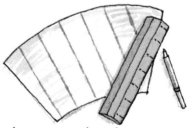

Flatten out the plastic. Use a ruler and pen to draw lines about 2cm (1in) apart. Cut along the lines.

Cut a point at one end of each strip, so it will stick easily into the compost. Tie in bundles with ribbon.

Painted pots

◁ A nice clay pot only needs its rim painted.

You can paint any sort of container. Ceramic paint (from art shops) is the best to use, but any paint will do.

▷ Work your way around the pot.

Paint the pot white first. This forms a good base and makes colours painted on top look brighter.

◁ Cut a kitchen sponge into pieces.

You could use a stencil to make patterns. Hold it against the pot – dab with a sponge dipped in paint.

Making a flower press

Making a collection of pressed flowers is one of the most interesting ways to learn about and identify plants. You can also use pressed flowers to make greeting cards, bookmarks and pictures.

You need stiff cardboard (from a box, for example); corrugated cardboard; newspaper; wrapping paper; a long ribbon; art knife; scissors; glue.

▽ The corrugated card allows air in so the plants dry and don't go mouldy.

Cut two pieces of stiff cardboard about 20cm (8in) square. Cut several sheets of newspaper and four squares of corrugated cardboard the same size.

Put glue around the edges of the stiff cardboard and stick each one onto a piece of wrapping paper, then cut them out. These two are your base boards.

▷ Press each handful of paper and card down firmly.

Put one base board covered side-down. Add six layers of newspaper, then a corrugated square. Repeat three times to make a pile.

Put the other base board on top of the pile, pretty side-up. Lift the pile up, then Place on the ribbon, then tie tightly, like a parcel.

▽ It takes about a week in a warm, airy place for the flowers to dry.

To press flowers, undo the ribbon, and lay them gently between layers of newspaper. Put the rest of the pile on top and tie up.

Bud

Buds are found at the end of stems and just below leaves. In winter, you can often recognise trees from the shape and arrangement of the buds.

Buds normally start to grow in spring and develop into a leaf, flower or stem.

△ Flower bud

▷ Filling up a compost bin to make a compost heap.

Bulb

A bulb is an underground part of a plant that is resting until conditions are right for growth. Bulbs store food and protect a baby shoot. As soon as they are given water and something to grow in, roots grow from the bottom and a shoot from the top.

▷ Bulbs come in many sizes.

Potting compost is bought from garden centres and used for growing plants in pots or containers. It is carefully made to a recipe that makes sure it holds air, water and plant food.

Cutting

A cutting is a piece of a plant, usually the tip of a stem, that once planted can make roots and grow into a new plant.

▷ A cutting planted in rooting compost and ready to take root.

Compost

There are different sorts of compost. Garden compost is made from lawn mowings, garden clippings and vegetable peelings from the kitchen. Mixed together and piled into a large container (compost bin) it rots down to make something rather like soil. Garden compost is rich in plant foods and good to dig into the soil and put around plants.

Dead-heading

If you remove fading flowers from a plant, it can't make seeds. This is called 'dead-heading' and often keeps a plant flowering for longer. A plant keeps producing flowers until they are allowed to set seed to make the next generation.

Drainage
For roots to be healthy they need water and air. When rain falls on the soil or you water a plant in a pot, some gets used, but the rest must be able to drain away. If it can't, then the soil becomes water-logged and the plant dies.

Deciduous
A bush or tree that drops its leaves in winter is described as deciduous. Before they fall, leaves often turn from green to rich orange, red and yellow colours.

Evergreen
An evergreen plant doesn't lose its leaves in winter, unlike a deciduous one. Evergreen trees and shrubs loose a few leaves all year round and replace them with new ones.

Evergreen ivy ▷

Fertilizers
Plants need food just like we do. But they prefer plant foods called nitrogen, phosphorus and potassium. Plants growing in pots and containers need regular feeding with fertilizers containing these plant foods to keep them healthy. Many different sorts are sold in granules, powders or liquids. Use an organic one as it's better for the environment.

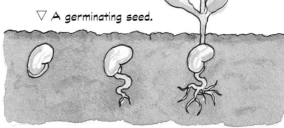
▷ If you add liquid feed to water you can do two jobs at once.

Flower
Flowers attract pollinators, such as birds and bees. They might be brightly coloured or sweet-smelling, or both! After pollination, a fruit or seed-pod grows with seeds inside.

△ A honey bee searches for pollen.

Germinate
When a seed is planted, it starts to grow roots, stems and leaves. This is called germination.

▽ A germinating seed.

Leaf
Most leaves are green and used to trap sunlight, which is turned into energy that helps a plant to grow.

Manure
Manure is made from straw and animal droppings from animals such as horses and cows. It is full of goodness and it doesn't smell horrible. Manure is forked into flower-beds and into planting holes. It is good for the soil and for plants.

Mulch
A mulch is a thick layer of material that is put around plants. Manure, compost or chopped bark make good mulches. A mulch stops weeds growing, feeds the soil and keeps moisture in the soil.

▽ Woodchips   ▽ Straw

Pollen
Pollen is a fine yellow dust found in flowers. It is carried on the stamens which is the male part of the flower. Bees often collect pollen and carry it to the stigma (female part) of another flower. This is called pollination.

Plant names
Plants like all living things have two names (rather like our Christian name and surname). The first is an everyday, or common name. The other is usually in Latin, which means that if you know the correct name you can talk about plants to someone in a different country, even if you can't understand their language.

Pruning
Pruning means cutting stems off a plant or tree. You may prune to remove dead branches or stems, or to give a plant a nice shape, or to encourage it to make more flowers.

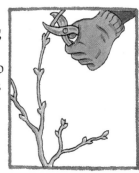

Roots
Roots are the anchor of a plant – they hold it firmly in the soil. Roots are also covered with tiny hairs that take in water and plant foods.

▽ The long runners of a strawberry plant grow into a new plant.

Runner
Some plants like strawberries and spider plants, make long, trailing stems called runners. At the end of each one, a little baby plant often develops. Once cut from the parent plant it will soon grow just as big.

Secateurs
Secateurs are gardener's scissors. They are tough and can be used for all sorts of jobs in the garden. They are good for pruning plants and cutting thick stems.

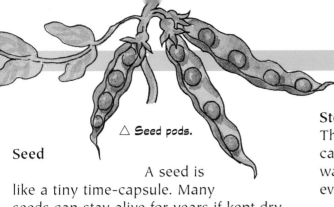

△ Seed pods.

Seed

A seed is like a tiny time-capsule. Many seeds can stay alive for years if kept dry and cool. Once water and soil are added, they will grow into a new plant.

Shrub

A shrub is a bush that will live for many years. It can be very large or quite small so make sure you find out how big a shrub gets before planting one in your garden.

The hebe is a very popular shrub. ▷

Sowing

When you put seeds into the soil to grow you are sowing them. You can sow seeds directly into the soil or into little pots indoors.

Stake

A stake is a sturdy, strong stick used to stop plants flopping over. They are useful for newly planted trees to stop wind damage and for plants such as delphiniums with tall flowers that break easily.

Stem

The stem is the part of the plant that carries the leaves and buds. It carries water and plant foods from the soil to every single leaf.

Thinning and pricking out.

Seeds are so small that we sow them close together. After seedlings have germinated they need to be spaced out so they get enough light. When they have three or four leaves move them to a bigger pot or plant outside at least 5cm (2in) apart.

Tree

Trees are plants with strong, woody stems called trunks. They have bark to protect them from the cold and pests and diseases. Trees can live for hundreds of years and are a valuable part of our environment.

Weed

Weeds are very clever and adaptable. They grow very fast, so if you don't take weeds out of pots and flower beds they soon smother all the plants around them.

▷ Spear thistle

Index

When you look through this index you may come across 'see' references, this leads you from one word to another which is more usually used in gardening, for example 'bush' see shrub. When you find a page reference which has a dash between the numbers following it, it means that you start at the first page number and read on until you come to the last number, for example, 33-34 means reading pages 33 and 34.